Art of Our Time

2

Art
of Our Time

The Saatchi Collection

Lund Humphries London

in association with

NEW YORK

Art of Our Time

Copyright © 1984 Lund Humphries Publishers Ltd
Published in 1984
(except in the United States of America) by
Lund Humphries Publishers Ltd
26 Litchfield Street   London WC2H 9NJ

ISBN 0 85331 477 2   paperback
ISBN 0 85331 481 0   casebound in boxed set of 4
                     volumes

Published in 1985 in the United States of America by
Rizzoli International Publications Inc
712 Fifth Avenue   New York NY 10019

ISBN 0–8478–0575–1   paperback

LC 84–61639

Designed by Herbert & Mafalda Spencer
Made and printed in Great Britain by
Lund Humphries Printers, London and Bradford

Published in four volumes:

Book 1

ANDRE BAER BELL FLAVIN HESSE JUDD LEWITT MANGOLD MARDEN MARTIN McCRACKEN MORRIS NAUMAN RYMAN SANDBACK SERRA TUTTLE

By Peter Schjeldahl

Book 2

ARTSCHWAGER CHAMBERLAIN SAMARAS STELLA TWOMBLY WARHOL

By Jean-Christophe Ammann Michael Auping Robert Rosenblum Peter Schjeldahl

Book 3

BASELITZ GUSTON KIEFER MORLEY POLKE SCHNABEL

By Rudi Fuchs Hilton Kramer Peter Schjeldahl

Book 4

BARTLETT BOROFSKY BURTON CLOSE FISCHL GOLUB JENNEY JENSEN LONGO MURRAY NUTT ROTHENBERG SALLE SHAPIRO SHERMAN WINTERS

By Prudence Carlson Lynne Cooke Hilton Kramer Kim Levin Mark Rosenthal Phyllis Tuchman

CLEMENTE

By Michael Auping

DEACON HODGKIN KOSSOFF SCULLY WILLING

By Lynne Cooke

List of Illustrations

Dimensions are given first in inches, then in centimetres.
Height precedes width precedes depth, unless otherwise indicated.

RICHARD ARTSCHWAGER

1
Mirror Painting
1962
Acrylic on celotex, formica and wood
60×31×10 (153×79×25)

2
Rocker I
1964
Formica on plywood, steel counterweight
62×26×28 (157×65×72)

3
Table with Pink Tablecloth
1964
Formica on wood
25¼×44×44 (64×112×112)

4
Mirror
1964
Formica
61×43×4 (155×110×10)

5
Long Table with Two Pictures
1964
Table: Formica on wood
33¾×96×22¼ (86×244×56)
Pictures: Acrylic on celotex with formica
Each: 42×32¼ (107×82)

6
Handle
1965
Formica
42½×13×12 (108×33×31)

7
Chair
1966
Formica
59×18×30 (151×46×77)

8
Expression Impression
1966
Acrylic on celotex
23½×30 (60×76)

9
Office Scene
1966
Acrylic on celotex
42×43 (106·7×109)

10
Upper Right Corner Hit
1969
Acrylic on celotex
23½×30 (60×76)

11
Bushes II
1970
Acrylic on celotex
23½×28¼ (60×72)

12
Library
1965
Acrylic on celotex
30×41 (76×104)

13
Untitled Interior
1973
Acrylic on celotex
60×46⅝ (152·4×118·4)

14
Interior (North)
1973
Acrylic on celotex
2 panels: Top 52¾×88½ (134×225)
Bottom 52⅛×88½ (133×225)

15
Interior (West)
1973
Acrylic on celotex
2 panels: Top 48⅞×75⅞ (124×193)
Bottom 50⅞×75⅞ (129·5×193)

16
Eight Rat Holes
1968/75
Acrylic on celotex
8 panels: (1) 23½×19 (59·5×48·5)
(2) 18×23 (45·5×58)
(3) 18×24 (46×61)
(4) 23×18 (58·5×46)
(5) 23×22 (58·5×56)
(6) 23×19 (58·5×48·5)
(7) 22×24 (56×61)
(8) 28½×23 (72·5×58)

17
Tower III (Confessional)
1980
Formica and oak
60×47×32 (153×120×81)

18
Book II (Nike)
1981
Formica
74×45¾×46 (188×116×117)

19
Rug and Window
1983
Acrylic on celotex
51½×51¾ (131×132)

JOHN CHAMBERLAIN

20
Captain O'Hay
1961
Welded auto metal
45 (114) high

21
Pure Drop
1982
Painted and chromium plated steel
135×72×36 (343×183×91·5)

22
The Arch of Lumps
1983
Painted and chromium plated steel
142×64×57½ (360·7×162·6×146)

23
Fenollosa's Column
1983
Painted and chromium plated steel
125½×53×47½ (318·8×134·6×120·7)

LUCAS SAMARAS

24
Untitled – October 23, 1960
1960
Pastel on paper
Sheet: 12×9 (30·5×23)

25
Untitled – February 16, 1961
1961
Pastel on paper
Sheet: 12×9 (30·5×23)

26
Untitled – August 14, 1961
1961
Pastel on paper
Sheet: 12×9 (30·5×23)

27
Untitled – August 14, 1961
1961
Pastel on paper
Sheet: 12×9 (30·5×23)

28
Untitled – Early November 1961
1961
Pastel on paper
Sheet: 12×9 (30·5×23)

29
Untitled – July 13, 1962
1962
Pastel on paper
Sheet: 12×9 (30·5×23)

30
Untitled – July 17, 1962
1962
Pastel on paper
Sheet: 12 ×9 (30·5 ×23)

31
Box No.4
1963
Wood construction, steel straight pins, nails,
hinges, razor blades, fork, plastic, sand, glass plate
and goblet, mosaic tiles, coloured wool yarn
Open: 18¹/₄ ×24¹/₂ ×11¹/₂ (46·5 ×62·5 ×29·7)

32
Box No.8
1963
Wood construction, wool yarn, photographs, wire,
glass lenses, plastic, stuffed bird
Closed: 11 ×15 ×8 (28 ×38 ×20)

33
Self Portrait Box
1963
Wood construction, red-white-blue wool yarn, steel
straight pins, 50 photographs of the artist, lead piece
Closed: 3³/₄ ×5⁷/₈ ×4³/₈ (9·5 ×15 ×11·2)

34
Shoe Box
1965
Wood construction, wool yarn, shoe, steel straight
pins, cotton, paint
10¹/₂ ×15¹/₂ ×11 (26·7 ×39·4 ×28)

35
Box No.49
1966
Wood construction, wool yarn, beads, plexiglass,
plastic, paint
Closed: 5× 12 ×9 (13 ×30·5 ×23)

35a
Chair Transformation No.20
1969/70
Corten steel
95 ×18 ×19 (241·3 ×45·7 ×48·3)

36
Room No.3
1968
Mirror on wood frame
108 ×108 ×108 (274 ×274 ×274)

37
Chicken Wire Box No.21
1972
Acrylic on chicken wire mesh
13⁷/₈ ×11³/₄ ×15 (35 ×30 ×38)

38
10/25/73
1973
SX 70 Polaroid
3 ×3 (7·6 ×7·6)

39
11/1/73
1973
SX 70 Polaroid
3 ×3 (7·6 ×7·6)

40
4/4/76
1976
SX 70 Polaroid
3 ×3 (7·6 ×7·6)

41
4/4/76
1976
SX 70 Polaroid
3 ×3 (7·6 ×7·6)

42
7/31/76
1976
SX 70 Polaroid
3 ×3 (7·6 ×7·6)

43
9/8/76
1976
SX 70 Polaroid
3 ×3 (7·6 ×7·6)

44
Box No.82
1976
Wood construction, steel straight pins, sculpmetal,
paint
17 ×12 ×10¹/₂ (43 ×30·5 ×27)

45
Box No.94
1976
Wood construction, wool yarn, steel straight pins,
acrylic, knives
13 ×13 ×26 (33 ×33 ×66)

46
Sculpture Table
1981
Gold plated bronze
41³/₄ ×51¹/₂ ×35 (106 ×131 ×89)

47
Sculpture Table
1981
Silver plated bronze
41³/₄ ×51¹/₂ ×35 (106 ×131 ×89)

48
Chair with Male – Female Entanglement II
1983
Gold plated bronze
33 ×17¹/₂ ×19 (83·8 ×44·5 ×48·3)

49
Head Group No.3
1983
Ink wash on paper
22 sheets, Overall: 96 ×132 (243·8 ×335·3)

FRANK STELLA

50
Joatinga I
1975
Lacquer and oil on aluminium
96 ×132 (240 ×330)

51
Steller's Albatross
1976
Mixed media on aluminium
120 ×165 (304·8 ×419)

52
Laysan Millerbird
1977
Mixed media on aluminium
83 ×123 ×15 (207·5 ×307·5 ×37·5)

53
Thruxton
1982
Mixed media on etched magnesium
109¹/₂ ×110³/₄ ×23 (273·8 ×277 ×57·5)

54
President Brand
1982
Honeycomb aluminium
121 ×101 ×78 (302·5 ×252·5 ×195)

55
Western Driefontein
1982
Aluminium and etched magnesium with mixed
media
120 ×100 ×80 (304·8 ×254 ×203)

56
Western Holdings
1983
Mixed media on aluminium
120 ×112 ×98 (304·8 ×280 ×245)

CY TWOMBLY

57
Untitled
1956
Oil, crayon, pencil on canvas
48^1/$_8$ ×69 (122·2 ×175·3)

57a
Untitled
1959
Oil, crayon, pencil on canvas
58 ×79 (147 ×200)

58
Leda and the Swan
1960
Oil, crayon, pencil on canvas
76^1/$_4$ ×80 (190·5 ×203)

59
Sahara
1960
Oil, crayon, pencil on canvas
80 ×110 (203 ×275)

60
Red Painting
1961
Oil, crayon, pencil on canvas
66 ×80 (165 ×203)

61
A Roma
1964
House paint, crayon, pencil on canvas
78^3/$_4$ ×82^1/$_2$ (200 ×206·3)

62
Untitled
1968
House paint, crayon on canvas
68 ×90 (170 ×225)

63
Untitled
1968
Oil, crayon on canvas
60 ×68 (150 ×170)

64
Untitled
1968
Oil, pencil on canvas
68^1/$_8$ ×87^7/$_8$ (173 ×216)

65
Untitled (Bolsena)
1969
House paint, oil, crayon, pencil on canvas
78^3/$_4$ ×98^1/$_2$ (200 ×250)

66
Untitled (Bolsena)
1969
House paint, oil, crayon, pencil on canvas
78^3/$_4$ ×98^1/$_2$ (200 ×250)

67
Untitled Grey Painting (Bolsena)
1969
Oil, crayon on canvas
78^3/$_4$ ×98^1/$_2$ (200 ×250)

There is no plate 68

ANDY WARHOL

69
Campbell's Soup Can
1962
Oil on canvas
20 ×16 (50·8 ×40·6)

70
Marilyn ×100
1962
Acrylic and silkscreen on canvas
81 ×223^1/$_2$ (205·7 ×567·7)

71
Triple Elvis
1962
Acrylic silkscreened on canvas
82 ×118 (208·3 ×299·7)

72
Elvis 49 Times
1962
Acrylic and silkscreen on canvas
80^1/$_2$ ×60 (204·5 ×152·4)

73
Double Disaster: Silver Car Crash
1963
Silkscreen on canvas
2 panels: 105 ×166 (266·7 ×421·6)

74
Blue Electric Chair
1963
Acrylic and silkscreen on canvas
2 panels: 105 ×160^1/$_2$ (266·7 ×407·6)

75
Tunafish Disaster
1963
Synthetic polymer paint and silkscreen on canvas
124^3/$_8$ ×83 (316 ×211)

76
Most Wanted Man No.11, John Joseph H.
1963
Silkscreen on canvas
2 panels: 48 ×80 (122 ×203·2)

77
Liz
1964
Synthetic polymer paint and silkscreen on canvas
40 ×40 (101·6 ×101·6)

78
Jackie
1965
Synthetic polymer paint and silkscreen on canvas
16 panels: 80 ×64 (203·2 ×162·6)

79
Atomic Bomb
1965
Silkscreen on canvas
104 ×80^1/$_2$ (264 ×204·5)

80
Flowers
1966
Acrylic and silkscreen enamel on canvas
81^3/$_4$ ×140^1/$_2$ (207·6 ×356·9)

81
Double Marlon
1966
Printers ink silkscreened on canvas
84 ×95^3/$_4$ (213·4 ×243·2)

82
Self Portrait
1967
Acrylic and silkscreen on canvas
72 ×72 (183 ×183)

83
Mao
1973
Acrylic and silkscreen on canvas
176^1/$_2$ ×136^1/$_4$ (448·3 ×346·1)

Biographical Notes

RICHARD ARTSCHWAGER

Born in Washington, DC, 1923
Education:
Cornell University, Ithaca, New York (BA)
Studied with Amedée Ozenfant
Lived in New Mexico
Lives and works in New York City

JOHN CHAMBERLAIN

Born in Rochester, Indiana, 1927
Raised in Chicago, Illinois
Education:
School of Art Institute of Chicago, Illinois, 1951–2
Black Mountain College, Beria, North Carolina,
1955–6
Recipient of Guggenheim Foundation Fellowship,
1966 and 1977
Awarded commission by Art & Architecture
Program of the United States General Services
Administration, 1978
Lives and works in Sarasota, Florida

LUCAS SAMARAS

Born in Kastoria, Macedonia, Greece, 1936
Family settled in West New York, New Jersey, 1948
Education:
Rutgers University, New Brunswick, New Jersey,
1955–9 (admitted on scholarship)
Columbia University, New York (studied art history
under Meyer Shapiro. Woodrow Wilson
Fellowship), 1959
Attended Stella Adler Theater Studio, 1960
Instructor at:
Yale University, New Haven, Connecticut (an
advanced sculpture seminar) 1969
Brooklyn College, New York, 1971–2
Awarded commission by Art & Architecture
Program of the United States General Services
Administration, 1976
Lives and works in New York City

FRANK STELLA

Born in Malden, Massachusetts, 1936
Education:
Phillips Academy, Andover, Massachusetts,
1950–4 (studied painting with Patrick Morgan)
Princeton University, New Jersey (studied painting
and art history with Stephen Greene and William
Seitz), 1954–8
Moved to New York City, 1958
Recipient of Skowhegan School Medal for Painting,
Maine, 1981
Lives and works in New York City

CY TWOMBLY

Born in Lexington, Virginia, 1929
Education:
Boston Museum School of Fine Art, Boston,
Massachusetts, 1948–9
Washington & Lee University, Lexington, Virginia,
1949–50
Art Students League, New York, 1950–1
Black Mountain College, Beria, North Carolina
(studied with Franz Kline and Robert Motherwell),
1951–2
Moved to Rome, 1957
Lives and works in Rome

ANDY WARHOL

Born (Andrew Warhola) in Forest City, Pennsylvania,
1930
Education:
Carnegie Institute of Technology, Pittsburgh,
Pennsylvania, 1945–9 (BFA)
Moved to New York City, July 1949
Awarded commission from architect Philip Johnson
to make mural *Thirteen Most Wanted Men* for New
York State Pavilion at New York World's Fair, 1964
Recipient of Independent Film Award, 1964
Lives and works in New York City

Jean-Christophe
Ammann

Richard Artschwager

Richard Artschwager's works can look deceptively simple, especially the sculptures, when, in fact, each work has been carefully conceived with the aid of many preparatory drawings. The artist often mentions his sketchbooks in which changes of meaning and extensions of meaning are documented.

Artschwager is both painter and sculptor. (He constructs his sculptures with his own hands, using his own tackle.) He also creates 'reliefs', in which he explores the transition from the third to the second dimension. He works from the premise that art, in particular sculpture and painting, is a perceived object. A commonplace, no doubt, for it is apparent to all. But there are many commonplaces in which the truth is so obvious that it conceals the real truth. (When John Cage incorporated silence into his works it was not in order to create emptiness but to substitute listening for hearing).

What is perceiving? It relates not only to the senses – touch, sight and sound – but also to their reflective capacity. In the early 1960s Artschwager started to use the hardboard celotex: its grey, coarse-grained texture presents an image in its own right, as he showed in 1964 in *Long Table with Two Pictures* (plate 5), in which he framed two uniform sheets of celotex, above a long table. The surface of the pictures, accentuated by the conspicuous frame, changes according to the movement of the spectator and the incidence of light.

A work of art is traditionally an artefact that is placed in an environment. In *Elevator,* a sculpture exhibited at the 1983 Whitney Biennale in New York, Artschwager sought to achieve the opposite: He wanted to create an environment which people could enter. The 'elevator' consists of a softly lit, spacious interior with two buttons, one for an ascending, the other for a descending sound. The object of perception ceased to be the sculpture and became the people inside and their interaction. We are all familiar with the situation in which one finds oneself in a lift with strangers. No one looks at anybody else: the gaze wanders, upwards or to the floor. There is always a sort of sheepish silence. *Elevator* addresses something fundamental in Artschwager's work, the psychological aspect of the spectator's perception. The involvement of the spectator does not come about by chance: Artschwager draws on real-life situations and experience.

In 1964 Artschwager made the sculpture *Tower I,* a piece for two spectators who can look into a slit on either side of a slender rectangular cube. One sees a sector, perhaps only the eyes, nose and mouth. We experience the world in sectors and try to generalise them, to cease seeing them merely as sectors. This work, with its two steps in front of the window slits, prompts us to be receptive, to modify prejudice or an over-hasty impression so as to match another understanding and another sensibility.

The starting point for *Long Table with Two Pictures* which also dates from 1964 was, in fact, *Seated Group* (charcoal, acrylic and celotex) dating from 1962. Artschwager's original idea was for four pictures. The table with its white formica surface is surmounted by two monochrome grey plaques of hardboard celotex framed in formica. Formica is a synthetic material available in a variety of colours, both monochrome and marbled. Artschwager uses it to simulate something that is not there, to evoke illusionistic effects, as in *Table with Pink Tablecloth* (plate 3), *Rocker I* (plate 2), or *Chair* (plate 7). Since he is interested in the artificiality of his sculptures, he uses colour in a way that intensifies the metaphorical perceptual content.

Tower III (plate 17) is an open confessional, a work for two people. The title reminds us of *Tower I*, which was also a work for two people. The piece made a frightening impression on me, primarily, perhaps, because it looks as though it has come from a factory where such objects are mass-produced. Imagine – an object made for the most intimate purposes created by mass production! Indeed, this subversive alliance of intimacy and the universal is a perennial interest for Artschwager. *Tower III* is a construction that stands adjacent to a wall. One side is for a kneeling person, the penitent; the other, a box for a seated figure, for the priest. Between them is a dividing wall, the upper part consisting of a wooden grille. A narrow shelf below the grille on either side can be used as an armrest, or alternatively the hands can hold on to it. Three red formica plaques, the only coloured highlights in the sculpture, are placed where they are needed for kneeling, sitting and putting the feet. *Tower III* is a work that divides and unites people, in which the voice is the mediating agent (rather than the eye through an arrow-slit, as in *Tower I*). For Artschwager, *Tower III* is neither a religious nor an anti-religious work. It operates as both a confessional and a sculpture: it is not an expression of a need to confess, simply a *metaphor* for something intimate that the artist seeks to communicate, in no matter what form.

Book I is a wooden construction that can be laid on a table, with a slight curve imitating the appearance of an open book. *Book III (Laocoön)* is a powerful construction for one person to kneel in and cling on to; one is tempted to say, to supplicate heaven and to hold fast. Between the elongated handles is a tall black rectangle. *Book III* is not really a further development from *Book I*. The work has something to do with the distance between the gripping hands and the black surface that meets the eye. The subtitle *Laocoön* pinpoints the meaning of the sculpture but does not add anything that it did not already contain. Laocoön put himself in danger when he took a firm stand. He begged the Trojans not to allow the horse into the city, but in vain, and he and his sons were strangled by the sea-serpent. One is always in danger of losing one's ground. There is a clear connection between standing firm and looking at the black surface: the more one loses oneself in the blackness (in the dark, in the nameless) the more powerfully one needs the handle. In a way that again harks back to the confessional, not metaphysically, but in a more general sense that has to do with holding fast to one's course.

Book II (Nike) (plate 18), is also a piece for one person and works in space like a pulpit. It is further development of the theme that began with *Book I*. In *Book I*, he freed the 'book' by using a support and gave it a socle, in front of which is a step. He gave the two halves of the 'book', and the 'book' itself, a steeper lateral tilt. The result is a work possessing a dramatic quality that Artschwager has felt to be similar to that of the Nike of Samothrace in the Louvre. Whereas *Tower III* communicates a sense of intimacy in a publicly accessible form, *Book II (Nike)*, more of a pulpit than a speaker's desk, is a place for public speaking, where rhetoric, intonation, transmission take place. *Book II (Nike)* will always need to be so positioned that it can make this point, but never in such a way that it loses its primary role as a sculpture in its own right.

A striking aspect of Artschwager's work is its timelessness. A Cubist painting by Braque or Picasso is easy to date; so are, for example, the works of Jackson Pollock. But Artschwager's works offer little scope for meaningful comparisons, especially those from 1964 onwards, which could have been created yesterday or could be created today. That at any rate is my feeling and I find it pleasing.

Michael Auping   **John Chamberlain**

'Once you get past the materials, you see what the insanity is. And the insanity is what art is about. It is the sharing of an insanity that hasn't been suppressed. If you were to play it out in life itself, you'd probably get yourself killed or put away. But in art it's looked up to, considered as a genuine piece of information.'
John Chamberlain

Like his art, Chamberlain's remarks often have a way of subverting conversation. They seem to refer to many things, while being strictly about Chamberlain, which is no doubt the reason Chamberlain continues to be one of our more interesting and illusive artists. Indeed, he claims the respect of a unique cross-section of America's post-war avant-garde: from David Smith to Andy Warhol to Donald Judd to Richard Serra to Julian Schnabel. He is, in a way, the proverbial artist's artist. A Stella often hangs in the museum director's office; a Chamberlain hangs in Stella's office.

Admiration for Chamberlain can be at least partially attributed to the fact that he has never settled into habit or allowed his street-smart approach to culture to become shrill or glib; a difficult task over a thirty year career. Wit and personality always overcome style in Chamberlain's work. He prides himself on walking a thin line between intellect and intuition. While Chamberlain is credited with translating Abstract Expressionism into sculpture, he has with few exceptions avoided the overly dramatic, often theatrical impersonations of anguish of the second and third generation expressionists. He is also seen as a precursor of Pop, but has not indulged himself in its easier ironies. His exploration of different materials and his insistence on allowing materials 'to do what they do best', aligns him to some extent with the Minimal and Post-Minimalists, but he has avoided the formulaic baldness that comes with the overly conceptualised.

As Duncan Smith recently put it, Chamberlain's sculptures are 'too ironic for Abstract Expressionism, too painterly for sculpture, too expressive for hard-edge, geometrical art, too junky for those hypnotized by streamlining, too 'real' for critics who detest social commentary'. Such a position makes for fascinating art, but stormy careers. Chamberlain's 1972 retrospective at the Guggenheim Museum 'provoked some conspicuous critical misunderstanding'. Indeed, among the pioneers of contemporary sculpture, Chamberlain remains one of the least understood by a broad public.

The irony of this is that Chamberlain is well-known among colleagues for his unpedantic character and down-to-earth lack of art historical pretentions. Chamberlain readily admits to having 'a sort of short education in the history of art'. One of the artist's most memorable statements to me was that: 'In art, gardening and sex there is no competition. And you don't need any schooling either.'

Born in Rochester, Indiana in 1927, Chamberlain began an initial career as a hairdresser in the years 1947–8. From hairdresser to sheet metal expressionist, Chamberlain's life, again like his art, is known for taking unexpected turns. In

Taken from an essay entitled *Art, Gardening and Sex: Notes on the Sculpture of John Chamberlain* prepared for this book and to be published in its entirety in 1985.

All comments by the artist quoted were in conversation with the author.

between these two points, he attended the school of the Art Institute of Chicago, where he began to study painting. Although he was there only a short time (1951–2), he left with a few key experiences. He particularly remembers being impressed by a de Kooning painting entitled *Excavation* (1950) and a group of Giacometti sculptures then installed at the museum. Upon repeated viewings, *Excavation,* which seemed very large to Chamberlain at first, appeared to get smaller, while the Giacomettis sustained their original sense of scale. He remembers that this experience helped to direct his attention toward sculpture.

It was a year at Black Mountain College in 1956, however, that was the catalyst for Chamberlain's renegade spirit, and apparently his particular approach to building form. Chamberlain attended Black Mountain in the final year of its twenty-three year existence as an experimental multi-disciplinary artistic environment. As Chamberlain describes it, 'I was there during the poetry regime'. Chamberlain is adamant that his aesthetic and process of working developed partly out of a literary model, nurtured through the poetry classes of Charles Olson and Robert Creeley, who espoused a kind of process-oriented poetry. 'They were all thinking the same thing', Chamberlain recalls, 'but they all had different estimates about how form was built. This fitted in with an attitude I had. I wanted sculpture to exist on its own terms.' In another interview Chamberlain discusses how the poetry helped inform his particular approach to assemblage: 'The parts that went into them (collages and reliefs) became pretty much like the words I'd collect back when I was a student of Charles Olson. I didn't particularly understand the words other than whether I liked the look of them, as they were printed, let's say. Rather than try to determine an attitude by saying something that you'd understand, I picked out words I liked to look at. So I made a collection of these words; not unlike this pile of scrap around the floor here.'

Chamberlain moved to New York around 1957. Although he is younger than the Abstract Expressionists, he has always maintained a great admiration for the ideas and ambiance associated with that style. He has on numerous occasions acknowledged the influence of de Kooning and Kline. He credits Kline with being the more influential of the two. From Chamberlain's remarks, it seems the impact of Kline's images had to do with the apparent sense of speed and power with which they were created and that this was, at the time, an important source of inspiration for Chamberlain: 'It had to do with the power and glory forever. The force, the velocity, that's what I got out of Franz. I thought it was swifter and harder in the terms of the '50s, it seemed to be more accurate for me, a reality, to be influenced by Kline rather than de Kooning.'

It does seem that the speed of the process was a factor in Chamberlain's early development. In discussing his early efforts at collage, the artist remarked: 'I could never learn to make collages. It turned out that what I needed was a staple gun. That allowed for the velocity, for the speed of the making. You just throw on the materials and the paper and staple them down.' It is interesting, however, that Chamberlain's works, on the whole, bear a far more specific resemblance to de Kooning's paintings in terms of a baroque interlocking of rounded planes and lines, as well as being kindred in palette.

Commenting on an exhibition of Pop Art that incorporated car parts, Alfred Barr remarked, 'Except the American woman, nothing interests the eye of the American man more than the automobile, or seems so important to him as an object of aesthetic appreciation'. These works are, of course, made of automobile parts, and this fact should not be left out of an assessment of Chamberlain's accomplishments. He has chosen an extremely loaded material with which to work, one that carries the baggage of political, sociological and personal associations; a difficult material from which to form a personal language. Ideas that he was reforming or attacking the American dream have haunted Chamberlain's work since he began working with auto parts in the late 1950s. When those associations faded, there were still others. The American automobile is a very personal object – we do things in it we would only do in our most private spaces – and Chamberlain has also had to transcend what he calls the 'That-looks-like-my-old-Mustang' syndrome. Exactly what Chamberlain's car parts 'mean' has been one of the more illusive factors in his work. Duncan Smith has most recently pointed out the differences and, at times, inconsistencies in thought regarding the presence of Chamberlain's materials. His own view offers a broad semiotic sweep: 'The stuff of precapitalist sculpture could draw from the earth's bounty of clay or stone whereas forged metal transforms its origins more radically. When ore assumes the form of a machine, nature's traces appear even more effaced. Conceivably all of man's work could be reduced to final causes, and nature claimed as one possible origin, so that cars spring to life as naturally as do flowers.' Or as Chamberlain baldly puts it, 'Michelangelo had a lot of marble in his backyard, so to speak, I had a lot of this stuff'.

Alfred Hitchcock usually put a red herring in his films in which the camera would focus on a situation or object that gave us the impression it was important to the plot. In the end, it wasn't, which gave the conclusion a larger sense of irony and surprise. Chamberlain's continued use of auto parts is a red herring of sorts, in that it is not the *idea* of the automobile that fascinates him as much as the resistance it presents physically and conceptually. At the same time, however, the equivocal tension between car junk and art is the Chamberlain trademark. This overlapping sense of abstraction, metaphor and the physical reality of his materials is most clearly understood in parallel to Johns' early *Flags* and Rauschenberg's *Combines.* All three artists have demonstrated a unique ability to allow a 'loaded' material or image to be itself and something else simultaneously. Obviously, one does not take a second or third look at a Johns flag, a Rauschenberg goat or a Chamberlain fender because they are just that, but because a particular intelligence was operating on them to the point that their associative qualities were nearly gone. As Chamberlain modestly puts it, 'Common material is what an artist should use because it doesn't get in the way of doing an uncommon thing'.

Four important evolutionary phases can thus far be seen in the development of Chamberlain's work. The first phase is represented by a transition from an essentially linear aesthetic influenced by the sculpture of David Smith to an emphasis on volume and the utilisation of automobile parts (*Shortstop,* 1957 has been identified by the artist as the first of his works to incorporate automobile parts).

Captain O'Hay, 1961 (plate 20) along with other works created in that year, such as *Jackpot* (collection Andy Warhol) and *Kroll* (collection Albright-Knox Art Gallery) represents a later point in this first phase. Such works may be considered the first flowering of Chamberlain's mature and recognisable style. Previous works evolved from thin, metal-rod constructions – such as *Clytie,* 1954 (collection of the artist) and *Rochester,* 1957 (collection of the artist) – to works in which metal rods wrap around car parts but still maintain a relatively shallow space – such as *Shortstop,* 1957 (collection Richard Bellamy) and *Redwing,* 1960 (collection Mr and Mrs Hubert Neumann) – and finally to works such as *Captain O'Hay,* in which lateral appendages billow out from and around a central and concealed space.

In a recent conversation, Chamberlain mentioned that *Captain O'Hay* was made in his Rockland County studio in New City, New York, approximately twenty-five miles from New York City. The work was completed shortly after returning from a trip to New Mexico, and he thinks it might be named after a bar in Taos. As Chamberlain remembers it, 'It was done with a group of works based on some of my experiences out there (the Southwest United States). It's kind of western-primitive.'

A second turning point in Chamberlain's work occurred in the later part of the 1960s and early 1970s, in which he temporarily abandoned the use of automobile parts, creating a series of diverse works by tying pieces of foam rubber, melting plastic and compressing aluminium foil, galvanised aluminium and paper bags. According to the artist, 'I was isolating the particular characteristic of my method – compression – by applying it to different materials'.

The third phase involves a return to sheet metal car parts and a renewed emphasis on wall reliefs, which began in the early 1960s with works such as *Dolores James,* 1962 (collection Solomon R. Guggenheim Museum) and *Mr Press,* 1961 (collection Donald Judd).

The emphasis in the fourth and most recent phase in Chamberlain's development is as yet not clearly defined. Among other events, it has involved a move from the Northeast to a large sprawling studio in Sarasota, Florida, where he has been working on a number of projects simultaneously: indoor and outdoor free-standing sculpture, small table-top works made from Tonka Toys, hand-coloured prints, wall reliefs, cast porcelain engine parts and a series of floor-hugging sculptures made from truck chassis titled the 'Gondola' series, individually named after American poets.

Pure Drop, 1982 (plate 21), *The Arch of Lumps,* 1983 (plate 22) and *Fenollosa's Column,* 1983 (plate 23) were made in the Sarasota studio. One aspect of Chamberlain's development has been to work in series, each series emphasising a different format and/or scale. The three aforementioned works are part of a series or 'family' of ten works made over a year and a half period. (The term family is perhaps appropriate because various constituent auto parts which help make up given works in the series were exchanged and used in other works in the series until they found their final place.)

This series is characterised by a number of factors. Each work is composed of rather broad sheets of metal, in most cases van hoods and door panels. They are also distinguished by tower-like vertical extensions. It is the first series to introduce clear sealants, which function to protect the metal as well as to create a crisper, more reflective surface. These works have been referred to as the 'giraffe series' by the artist's assistants because they introduce the technique of sandblasting patterns into the painted surfaces of the sheet metal.

Pure Drop was the third work to be completed in the series. It consists of approximately fourteen parts. According to Chamberlain, *Pure Drop* 'came together the quickest. It's pretty simple. There are just a few parts that do a whole lot. It has a good stance: dramatic and formal.' The work is named after a bar in Dublin.

Pure Drop and *The Arch of Lumps* (the fourth work to be created in the series) are indicative of Chamberlain's recent *modus operandi* regarding surface treatment. Both works support three types of painting: the original paint of the auto parts; additional industrial paints applied with a compressor by Chamberlain's assistant; and graffiti-like patterns applied by Chamberlain with a spray can. Some of the parts that make up *Pure Drop* have as many as five coats of paint.

The Arch of Lumps was originally placed in a portable sculpture garden behind Chamberlain's studio, and later brought indoors. The title may derive from two possible meanings. As Chamberlain remarked, 'It's a pretty lumpy piece'. Given the artist's penchant for wordplay, one might assume the artist sees an arch as an elegant lump-like form. It has also been suggested, however, that *The Arch of Lumps* is Chamberlain's Vietnam War Memorial.

Fenollosa's Column, created sometime after the aforementioned works, is coloured predominantly by original car paint. One exception is the abstract calligraphy running up and down the slender tower-like form. The artist has recently devoted a notebook to this personalised writing cum drawing. According to Chamberlain's welder, who upon seeing the addition of these markings on the sculpture asked if it was the day's baseball scores, Chamberlain responded, 'No. It's the story of Iran–Iraq.' At the time, Iran and Iraq were headlining the news. The title, however, refers to Ernest Francisco Fenollosa, an orientalist and poet. As his literary executor, the poet Ezra Pound (who Chamberlain also named a recent sculpture after) used Fenollosa's notes to produce some of his most influential poetry.

Peter Schjeldahl   **Lucas Samaras**

To seek discussions of Lucas Samaras in critical collections and anthologies avails little. He almost isn't there. And yet he has been emphatically *there* in the serious art and art world of the last quarter-century, a constant presence exerting an intermittent, often startling pressure on those of acute sensibility. It's not merely that he is an 'artist's artist' – though he is that, routinely acknowledged as kindred by a wide variety of painters and sculptors. Samaras's reputation cuts across many frontiers in professional and public circles of American art. He is regarded, if not with universal admiration, at least with a mixture of affection and vigilance that might be merited by a splendid pet which has been known to bite. But he is regarded, for the most part, wordlessly, as if his work were too obvious or too ineffable – or both – for words. The truth is that Samaras's art is so devised that it can stop practically any critical discourse dead in its tracks. Not surprisingly, discourse has detoured around him.

Samaras had a harrowing childhood in his native Macedonia, during World War II and the Greek civil war, and came to America in 1948 at the age of eleven. In the late 1950s he attended Rutgers University, then a hotbed of heterodox avant-garde activity; Allan Kaprow, later the doyen of 'Happenings', was a teacher. He then studied art history with Meyer Schapiro at Columbia for three years. Meanwhile – reclusive and virulently narcissistic – he led his life and made his art almost exclusively in a tiny bedroom of his parents' apartment in the dilapidated city of West New York, across the Hudson River from Manhattan. When his parents returned to Greece in 1964, Samaras eased his transition to independence by reconstructing his bedroom in the Green Gallery and living in it for the course of, literally, a one-man show. When we deal with Samaras we are dealing with almost unimaginable extremes – held in perfect, calculated tension – of the sophisticated and the infantile. No other artist of the 1960s at once so thoroughly grasped the era's stylistic issues and so perversely defied its expectations.

Samaras is an avatar of the 'weird' personality in art, the individual who becomes an artist not for a vocation but for a therapeutic outlet and a substitute life. There is one in every class in every art school, probably going nowhere. What sets Samaras apart – as it also does, say, Gilbert & George – is extraordinary talent brought under extraordinary control. He confronts viewers with the superior, enchanting, somewhat frightening power of creativity that plays by its own rules and, moreover, systematically contradicts ordinary notions of the game. Serpent-subtle, Samaras has seduced response and traduced analysis in a hundred ways. Why does anybody stand for it? Perhaps because such subversion symbolically breaches the barrier – a construct of anxiety and shame – between the private and the public, the unspeakable and the hypocritical, in society. How else to explain the air of gleeful festivity, of dionysian intermission from the norm, that seems to accompany every museum or gallery show of Samaras's work?

Samaras is frank about his competitive relation to the art world of his time, starting with the *macho* Abstract Expressionists of the 1950s. He took up pastels in those days, he once told me, in reaction to the prevailing fashion for 'huge things or public gestures' and the idea that 'to become a man you had to do womanising and drinking and to use a certain kind of language'. Pastels 'had a connection to intimacy. You didn't think of drunken people doing them.' Samaras's remarks fit the feeling of the seven early pastels here (plates 24–30), which are delicate and sumptuous without being in the least genteel or charming. Exquisiteness, for him, is a way of exercising psychological dominance, by beguiling rather than browbeating. His hundreds of pastels – like his later 'Autopolaroids' (plates 38–43) – are a phantasmagoria of extremely specific subjective transformations. Each draws the willing viewer into its particular emotional whirlpool, its particular obliteration of distinctions between outside and inside, world and self. A dose of this stuff can make the grandiosity of 'huge things or public gestures' seem pretty futile.

Self-portraiture, of a complex sort, is a subtext of all Samaras's art, including his remarkable 'Boxes' of the 1960s (plates 31–35) – the work for which he is best known. The 'self' portrayed is more a psychic substance than an individual identity. You can look at everything Samaras has made and still know approximately nothing about him 'as a person', though quite a lot about him as a black magician. The gorgeous materials, textures, colours, and craftsmanly touches of the boxes function rather like the come-hither odours of a carnivorous flower, the kind that induces insects to explore a container which, as it turns out, is for them. Consider the photographs of Samaras in *Box No.8* (plate 32), two of them ornamented with attractive weaving and braiding and two of them lacerated. Each, that is, comes 'signed' with a particular activity of the artist's hand, his 'touch'. ('To sign' is to speak the language of the deaf, often with hand before face; and no set of actorly gestures is more eloquent than those bringing hand to face.) The visible but passive face and the active but absent hand together form a sort of feedback loop of exhausting intensity.

People who dismiss Samaras's art – as 'precious', to note their usual pejorative – often betray a want of attentiveness by lumping it with the lapidary Surrealism of Joseph Cornell. There is a vast difference between Samaras's boxes and those of Cornell. A true eccentric, the latter made art to memorialise his extravagantly sublimated yearnings – erotic affects that got invested in astronomical charts and defunct opera singers. From the viewer, he wanted tender complicity. Samaras, even when his work most resembles Cornell's, is far more detached; he isn't parading his sensibility, because in a real sense he doesn't have one. What he has is an intention to excite viewers, drawing them into sensual, fantasising relationships with his creations, his simulacra. In this respect, Samaras bears less affinity to Surrealism than to the artistic philosophy of Minimalism, with its displacement of meaning from the artist's 'expression' to the viewer's experience. His work refers us to no dreamy netherworld, but presents us with a blunt proposition of dalliance, which we are free to accept or decline.

Room No.3 (plate 36), a walk-in mirrored environment replete with nasty mirrored spikes, epitomises Samaras's devilish strategy. Beautiful and tempting, it promises a bit of fun; and its infinitely reflecting interior is indeed entertaining. What with visual disorientation and the spikes, however, one is almost certain, though moving ever so cautiously, to do oneself some bodily hurt. Knowing this –

perhaps after seeing other people emerge from the thing bruised and whimpering – one will no doubt elect to forego the pleasure, with a whiff of the sour regret that comes with following 'better judgment' in matters of love. No sentimentality of the Unconscious here. The metaphor of lure and pain – Odyssean siren song and shipwreck – is comically palpable. This metaphor, or syndrome, is consistent throughout Samaras's art, enacted on some level in even his gentlest pastels and most modest objects. Taken as a whole, Samaras's work makes the profound suggestion that this erotic mechanism is a secret engine of *all* art.

Samaras's recent bronze sculptures (plates 46–48) and mask-like face drawings (plate 49) are a malign puppet show. The bronzes, patinated gold or silver, are his most traditional-looking work in three dimensions and exploit apparent conventionality in much the way that his pastels have: giving a superficial reassurance which, after some imaginative participation, the viewer discovers to be misleading. (By appearing affably goofy, the paper faces similarly disarm, only to involve one in a fairly violent repertoire of crazed emotions.) The sculptures incorporate their pedestals in the form of cast-bronze, vernacular-style tables or chairs, evoking domestic interiors inconvenienced by straying bric-a-brac. Obviously out of place, the objects invite the perfunctorily assessing glance with which we look at something to see where it belongs. Were we indeed to come upon them in this way, our response would likely be a stab of strong disquiet, followed by curiosity, followed by a deeper feeling of disturbance. These little statues belong not in a world of cold things but in a mental realm of molten obsession, a savannah of death-fears and sexual deliriums. Their frozen writhings catch us up in a turmoil of aimless associations and the kind of fascination we might feel while gazing into a box of snakes that finally, with a shudder of decision, we slam shut.

Samaras, let us say, is a barbaric Byzantine – a paradoxical rubric he earns by being elaborately refined in a crude cause. It's as if he understood everything about artistic formality except its civilised purpose, which is to be a protocol by which artist and viewer acknowledge each other's autonomous roles. Samaras clambers over midnight battlements, knife in teeth, to slaughter all such gentlemen's agreements. His 'otherness' is implacable, insatiable, and completely unsympathetic. Yet something in us – in me, at any rate – cheers him on. Didn't Freud teach us that we can never hope to stop hating, with excellent reason, the constraints of civilisation? In a civilisation ominously lacking rituals for such primordial resentment, a Samaras in an art gallery is an oddly stirring sight. It is art, but also something less and more than art. It is just, harmlessly, a thing, but a thing that one is somehow loath to turn one's back on. Its stillness seems unreliable. One half expects it to snarl or purr. What does it do, one wonders, after hours, when the doors are locked, the streets outside are empty, and the lights are all turned out?

Robert Rosenblum   **Frank Stella**

Only a decade ago, in the 1970s, Frank Stella was thought of mainly as the artist who had made history in 1959 by stopping Abstract Expressionism dead in its tracks. He did it with a series of path-breaking paintings of numbing economy and symmetry, in which everything that had to do with impulse, movement, pleasure had been banished. Like a monk taking vows of purity, asceticism, and absolute order, he redefined the rectangular area of the painter's canvas with a sequence of variations on a theme of repeated black stripes systematised in patterns of imprisoning constraint. It seemed a point of no return, the rockbottom statement of a zealous reformer who would clean out the Augean stables of painting and make it all start again with the cleanest and most colourless of slates.

But the septet of Stellas in the Saatchi Collection offers what first looks like the work of a totally different artist who, so to speak, had conquered his anorexia but replaced it with an acute case of bulimia. Here, an overwhelming abundance of shapes, colours, scribbles, movements is not only greedily devoured but, even more miraculously, digested. Although we may begin to read this sequence of works, from 1975 to 1983, as we might read paintings hung on a wall and looked at head on, the conventions of easel painting are gradually undermined here, even in a literal way. None of these works, in fact, is executed on canvas, whose porousness has been replaced by aluminium and magnesium grounds that offer a tough, material surface. Instead of absorbing us imaginatively into the soft, absorbent depths of painted fictions, as does canvas, these works literally invade our space with ever more palpable thrusts and cutting edges. Indeed, by 1982–3, these metal structures had become so sharp, so jagged, so protrusive that we approach them with the physical caution registered at the sight of monumental fragments of shrapnel. Blocking traffic and slowing our step, these ten-foot high objects seem nevertheless to have burst into our space from what was once a rectangular easel painting.

This amazing evolution can be read through the Saatchi Collection beginning with *Joatinga I* of 1975 (plate 50), one of the Brazilian series. This was the first of Stella's series to use metal exclusively as the base for lacquered surfaces covered with a variety of drawn and painted colours, and as such, also the first to fuse not only visually, but in the most literal, material terms, the traditions of metal relief sculpture with those of drawing and easel painting. In *Joatinga I*, the alternation of thin, long strips and flat, broad planes conjures up the ghost of what might once have been a framed abstract painting, but one which has been exploded and then reassembled as a restless jigsaw-puzzle that appears to be bursting at every seam. Stella's familiar joining of the opposites of extreme discipline and centrifugal energies permeates this unpredictable splaying of like and unlike fragments. The emphatic horizon line below insists on law and order but, like the other components, tilts unexpectedly away from the drum-tight flatness of painting on canvas, at least as defined so single-mindedly by Stella himself at the beginning of his career. Liberation is afoot, too, in the surprising passages of thick and thin, long and short scribbles and doodles, whose graffitist instincts are immediately held in check by the regimented geometries of the underlying structure and the razor-sharp precision of the enclosing edges. And rebellion can be felt as well in the flamboyant colours, whose tropical flavour of a Latin-American fiesta, appropriate to the Brazilian motifs that link the titles of this series, moves to the opposite pole from the ascetic, depressive character of the early black paintings, whose titles usually referred to the dark and seamy sides of New York life. Plain song has been replaced by the carioca.

By 1976–7, this topsy-turvy rejection of his own foundations (not to mention of the prevailing 1970s period style of Minimalism and Conceptualism, which more often evoked a mathematician's or philosopher's study than a carnival in Rio) reached even more extravagant extremes in the Exotic Birds series, represented by two works in the Saatchi Collection. The earlier of the two, *Steller's Albatross* of 1976 (plate 51), whose title wittily strikes up a nominal acquaintance between Stella himself and the eighteenth-century naturalist, Georg Wilhelm Steller (who discovered and gave his name to many species of exotic birds), immediately announces the main themes which Stella varies in this series. Here, the major components are of a far wilder, more baroque character than in the Brazilian series, providing virtually a draughtsman's inventory of standardised tools, floating templates that range from the right-angled clarity of picture frames to wriggling flurries of sharp-edged French curves. Stella's ongoing tug-of-war between the forces of order and rebellion, already clashing in the Brazilian series, is daringly escalated here. The centre field is so explosively centrifugal that we feel the forms are caught mid-air in a gravity-defying high-wire act. Yet as an instant control over these pictorial acrobatics Stella straitjackets them in a pair of frames. The smaller inner frame tilts forwards and backwards, as if temporarily unhinged by this whirlwind energy; whereas the larger outer frame holds tight, finally constraining what looks like a revolt of sweeping brushstrokes that have suddenly materialised into palpable forms and are about to hurtle out of the shallow, box-like frame which momentarily contains them. This unleashing of energy pertains to both structure and ornament. The bold collisions of swirling French curves and elliptical strips define the restless skeleton of this work, a skeleton which, following Stella's usual habits of exploring carefully plotted themes and variations, is used for three different sizes of the same composition, each one of which is different in colour and in decorative embellishment. The underlying form is clearly displayed as primary, whereas the turbulent marks of seemingly impulsive surface agitation, from lean doodles to frothy brushstrokes, appear, together with the brash colours, as secondary enhancements to the bones of the image. In this, Stella almost revives the traditions of French academic theory, which would give priority to the enduring aspects of line and composition over such literally superficial and ephemeral matters as colour and brushstroke. Finally, then, the image of spontaneity here is a deception. No less than in the black paintings, the iron fist of Stella's intellect rules.

Often, in fact, the Exotic Birds series appears to be restatements and, as it were, corrections of the domain of Abstract Expressionism which Stella had attempted to annihilate so definitively in his black paintings of 1959. In the second example of this series in the Saatchi Collection, *Laysan Millerbird* of 1977 (plate 52), we also feel this resurrection of the pictorial language of de Kooning and Pollock translated into Stella's own obsessive fusion of method and madness. Here, works like Pollock's *Blue Poles* and the classic de Koonings of the 1950s seem to be recreated in Stella's expanding universe. Again, this work at first may look as reckless in spirit and execution as the mythical ideal of an Abstract Expressionist painting, yet it is, in fact, the largest variation upon a rigidly predetermined structure that exists in other, smaller formats; and the dominant shapes, for all their buoyant, whiplash energies, are as strictly codified as the hard-edged stripes and arcs which formed the vocabulary of Stella's first decade of painting in the 1960s. And once more, a prodigious variety of minor surface variations that would venerate muscular, impulsive execution in the de Kooning–Pollock vein embellishes the rigorously preordained composition. We realise what Stella meant when he put down the most recent wave of graffiti-inspired artists by saying that they had nothing worthwhile to draw their graffiti on.

Only historical hindsight could tell us that Stella would go on to create, if possible, even more luxuriant and dynamic works than these, as evidenced in the Saatchi Collection by a late example of the Circuit series, *Thruxton* of 1982 (plate 53). Named, like the others, after an international race track and thereby continuing the inspiration behind much of Stella's art (as well as one of his major passions in real life, sports cars and motor races), *Thruxton* ought to be a visual disaster, an indigestible glut that fuses a serpent's nest of labyrinthine circuits, a splintered explosion of every colour in the plastic rainbow, a *horror vacui* of honeycomb patterns and wild graffiti that seem refugees from the New York subway. Yet miraculously, this teeming chaos finally clicks into place, a tense but ultimate equilibrium between warring major and minor shapes, between the careening energies of endless serpentine movement and the restricting power of a rectangular format that, as in a huge altarpiece by, say, Rubens gives us a grand measure of rule against which to experience a turmoil of figural movement. Such analogies, in fact, are quite to the point, since Stella, in the early 1980s, was studying ever more closely the masters of sixteenth- and seventeenth-century painting as preparation for his Charles Eliot Norton lectures delivered at Harvard during the academic year 1983–4. In these he treated the issues of illusionistic depth created by the old masters and the problems of reinstating, within the flattened, airless spaces of abstract art, that sense of dynamic, muscular forces which came so easily to artists like Michelangelo, Caravaggio, and Rubens who used the human figure to create a living, breathing space. Such lofty ambitions, surveying the entire history of art, are set by Stella as goals for his own abstract paintings, which, like *Thruxton*, can not only make us think that the spirit of the Book of Kells has been reincarnated in the 1980s, but which, we feel, might hold their own even in the company of Delacroix's *Death of Sardanapalus.* Stella's unleashing and recapturing of epic energy recalls the noblest historical precedents.

To attain this, Stella had literally to burst out of the confines of an abstract art of two dimensions, colliding head-on with the medium of sculpture. Thinking about it in retrospect, it is hardly surprising that in the most recent works represented in the Saatchi Collection, three from the South African Mine series, the three-dimensional impulse that literally ruptured the vestiges of a pictorial format in the earlier works has now taken over entirely, metamorphosed into huge physical presences that emerge as monumental sculptures. Of this trio, *President Brand* of

1982 (plate 54) is perhaps the most hybrid, the emphatic fragment of an immense metal frame in the background recalling the insistent rectilinear edges of the Exotic Birds series. Yet the dominance of raw metal over painted and drawn surfaces as well as the harsh exposure of the interior weave of ragged metal edges that look as though they had been torn apart by a titan, already tilt the balance clearly toward the sculptural side of Stella's coin. Even though we may still read this mainly as a relief, it is a relief we can almost walk or bump into, so physically protuberant are its arced and looping shapes. The other two works of the series represented here, *Western Driefontein* of 1982 (plate 55) and *Western Holdings* of 1983 (plate 56) are more assertively, even dangerously three-dimensional, evoking Stella's friend John Chamberlain's crushed automobile sculptures of the 1950s and similarly employing metal detritus, the studio remnants of actual cast-off metal sheets used in the fabrication of tidier Stellas, including prints. This new direction yields more precarious, genuinely improvised results than the earlier series with their predetermined maquettes; and for all their colossal dimensions, they have almost the character of experimental studies, in which a heroic, unexpected equilibrium is achieved by a giant toying with the kind of gargantuan metal fragments generally left to fossilise in garbage dumps. That we still find, as in *Western Holdings*, painted and drawn passages that seem excerpted from the Exotic Birds and Circuit series is a tribute to the underlying continuities of Stella's art, a reference to his own immediate past. His next steps, however, remain unpredictable, no mean feat in a century when even the greatest artists have often been content to cultivate year after year the gardens of their first maturity. But we can, at least, predict that whatever new assaults Stella will make on our preconceptions about painting versus sculpture, good taste versus bad taste, chaos versus tyranny, the results, once we look backwards, will appear inevitable.

Robert Rosenblum **Cy Twombly**

The earliest Twombly in the Saatchi Collection transports us swiftly to the New York City of 1956, the place and the time that this untitled canvas (plate 57) was painted and scrawled upon. As the work of a 28-year-old, trying to find his identity in a territory occupied by the heavyweight authority of the likes of de Kooning and Pollock, it is a triumph. Bowing respectfully to these ancestral figures, it nevertheless speaks with its own voice. To be sure, the flavour of the New York School is everywhere apparent: the veneration of ragged, graphic impulse; the staking out of a field of teeming, perpetual motion, where traditional structures of major and minor, central and peripheral are challenged; and the reduction, as in so many works of de Kooning, Pollock, Kline, and Motherwell, to a language of black and white. Yet we immediately sense not discipleship, but a uniquely personal flavour. The elbow and shoulder movements of de Kooning and Pollock are replaced by a gentler calligraphy of wrist and finger. The raucous, colliding tracks of movement give way to a more muted, whispered ambience, as if we were experiencing through many veils of memory the record of some earlier actions and thoughts that had gradually been effaced both by long exposure and by later overlays of graffiti. Indeed, though the works of Pollock and de Kooning tend to speak in the present tense of an immediacy of visual and emotional outpourings, Twombly's canvas already speaks in a kind of layered past tense, in which we recognise long-ago beginnings and erasures, near-invisible strata that lie below the surface like ghost memories of earlier impulses. In a way which may be more than fortuitous, given Twombly's close friendship with Rauschenberg (they even had a two-man show in New York in 1953), this canvas recalls Rauschenberg's notorious act of patricidal exorcism, his wilful erasure in 1953 of a de Kooning drawing, an act whose results would symbolically and literally annihilate the forceful, animate presence of de Kooning's lightning-bolt drawing style and reduce it to a shadowy memory in the historical past.

Twombly's untitled canvas of 1956 can, of course, be associated as well with other earlier works that liberate calligraphic impulse for a wide spectrum of effects, whether the fine threaded webs spun out so quietly and exquisitely by artists hailing from the Pacific Northwest like Morris Graves and Mark Tobey, or the grander, international Surrealist tradition of believing that unedited doodles might convey deeper psychological truths than would more premeditated styles of drawing. Nevertheless the effect here remains very much that of New York, 1956, not only in terms of the echoes of the reigning Abstract Expressionist masters, but also in terms of a sensibility to that derelict but pulse-quickening urban environment which also nurtured Rauschenberg so richly in the 1950s, a microcosm of infinite density where every city wall and public sign might be defaced by layer after layer of random scribbles, a chaotic fossil deposit of psychological detritus comparable to a scrap heap of discarded automobile parts. And here, within this Lascaux of the twentieth century, tantalising suggestions of letters and words surface and disappear, illegible brambles that leave traces of lost or as yet unformed inscriptions. But if these are only graphological phantoms that throw us back to the origins of written language, there is at least no mistaking, in the upper left-hand corner, Twombly's own name and the date, 1956, a longhand scrawl which already seems to be vanishing behind a smudge of white paint that threatens eventually to efface the artist's very signature.

For among the other triumphs of Twombly's sensibility is the sense of seizing an organic world of change and process, at once rapid, attuned to the pursuit of a private impulse, and of long duration, attuned to what feels like decades and centuries of public historical layering, comparable to an archaeological site of multiple strata. Note, incidentally, that this ability to create layers of temporal resonance recalls that of another New York friend of Twombly's in the 1950s, Jasper Johns, who, in that decade in particular, through techniques of dense encaustic and just-visible underlays of the daily newspaper, could evoke a similar aura of historical accretion, in which the literally multi-layered surfaces convey a quality of survival and potential change that reaches nostalgically back into the past and forward to a future where messages that lie deep beneath these painted strata may either be more fully revealed or may disappear entirely.

This poetic character, drawn to meditations like those of a romantic wanderer upon things past, may well have seemed displaced in the perpetual present of New York's anti-historical tempo; and with hindsight, it seems right and inevitable that Twombly would become an American expatriate living in that world of maximum historical memory and mystery, the Mediterranean. A resident of Rome since 1957, and a traveller in both Spain and North Africa, Twombly seems to have absorbed the magic and the myths of both the classical world and its outlying exotic terrains. In *Sahara* of 1960 (plate 59), the signature in the lower right is like a private variant of an ancient Roman inscription, beginning with the artist's personal scrawl for name and place, but then dating it with Roman numerals MCMXXXXXX, as if Twombly were reincarnating some ancient historian and traveller, a modern Herodotus who explores the North African desert which here surfaces and again vanishes in the uncertain recall of a voyager's memory. Echoing the sketchbooks of earlier artist-travellers in North Africa, such as Delacroix, Twombly's canvas is a loose-jointed composite of a tourist's notations about sights, facts, and feelings. The faintly inscribed jottings range from spare strokes of blue crayon which may evoke the limpid sky of the desert, to diagrammatic fragments which seem to chart, topographically, the contours of distant hills, to elementary numerical sequences (1, 2, 3, 4, 5, 6, 7 . . .) which, as in the work of Johns may rejuvenate the magic of primitive commensuration. And here and there other words, images, symbols surface palely in these hazy souvenirs – suggestions of shrubby landscape; rounded forms that conjure up female anatomies; an unexpected node of overlapping intense colours that may shroud the memory of a gorgeous native costume; a passage of cubic geometries that may describe some rudimentary stepped architecture; a startling inscription, 'A Bubble of Beauty/ to Fragonard for Sappho', attached to a swollen, eroticised shape; and much, much more. A field of nostalgic free-associations, but all oriented to the same desert motif, quivers immaterially before our eyes in a strange language where shapes and symbols are only beginning to congeal and where wide and low framing rectangles, as in the sequence at the right, begin to offer some preliminary constraint of reason in which to grasp, as in the imagined rectangular form of a drawing or canvas, the horizontal infinities of the desert.

The archaism of Twombly's imagination, in which everything regresses to its mysterious birth pangs, can rekindle, too, pictorial traditions of illustrating classical myths, whose waning vitality in our own century generally required the genius of a Picasso to be temporarily sparked back to life. But in Twombly's introspective musings, this great, if moribund Western heritage seems reborn, as in the 1960 *Leda and the Swan* (plate 58), one of his many meditations on this venerable erotic metamorphosis which, in its coupling of Leda with Jupiter in the form of a swan, is at once carnal and ethereal, a fusion of the most physical sexuality with a white-winged airborne fantasy of Mallarmé-like frailty. Perhaps the memories of Correggio's or Leonardo's visions of Leda set off Twombly's own meditations on this theme, which, in this canvas, merge words and images to recreate the wonder of the Greek narrative, as if it had just been invented in some ancient poet's mind or illustrated by the very first artist of the classical world. The protagonists are present both as crudely inscribed words, as in a written fragment from an archaeological site where the tale was sacred, and as rudimentary ideograms, in which the profile of the long-necked bird, framed as in a hieroglyphic, is opposed to a softer, ovoid form, Leda, set beside a pool, and surrounded by suggestions of orifices and rounded anatomies. Below, a flurry of numbered, featherlike forms and a more intense reddened nexus of organic parts convey the physical encounter of, in Yeats's phrase, 'A sudden beat of wings'. And typically, other elementary motifs surface as weathered graffiti, from the implication of some primitive system of mensuration above, as if the first illustrator of this myth were marking out the dimensions of his image; to the suggestion of a framed landscape setting at the upper right; to the inventory, centre right, of crayon colours that would be used to give erotic pungency to this otherwise ghostly recall of the most sensual of myths.

Such whispers of colour generally seem repressive elements in Twombly's work, but on rare occasions, they can surface in surprisingly visceral exposures that play on moods of sexual and emotional violence. *Red Painting* of 1961 (plate 60) is one of these canvases in which we feel that the muffled sensuality of such earlier works as the untitled canvas of 1959 (plate 57a), whose drama seems concealed behind scrims of white paint, has suddenly burst its floodgates in a ragged clash of reds so intense by Twombly standards that we respond to it as to the bloody aftermath of a psychic or erotic battle. That there seems to be so private, so one-to-one a correlation between the artist's personal experience and the impulsive, associational character of his art is one of the many ways in which Twombly perpetuates, particularly in a painting like this, the tradition of Gorky's late work, where the most fluid, multi-layered paint surfaces are activated by gossamer linear traces and by sudden blossoms or wounds of colour that, we feel, record directly graphs of personal memory and emotion. And we feel this intensely, too, in more fragile and oblique works like *A Roma* of 1964 (plate 61) and an untitled canvas of 1968 (plate 62) where we almost discern the components of an autobiographical narrative, flickering entries in a private journal that may suggest glimmers of erotic longing or encounter within the smudged environment of number and letter graffiti that allude to the specifics of time and place.

Often, too, Twombly will return to what becomes for him, in this domain of the most ephemeral daydreams, a recurrently disciplinarian image, as if he were regaining control of his meandering, spiderweb doodles, the better to liberate them once again. This is the case here in four untitled works of 1968–9, two of which (plates 62, 64) repeat the obsessive rhythms of an archaic exercise in the rudiments of cursive script, as if we were looking at the archetype of all classroom blackboards on which a teacher first taught us the principles of penmanship. Indeed, the colours, or rather, non-colours – slate-grey and chalky white – underscore this association, as does the sense of approaching a ruled, horizontal order, as in a primitive system of writing. This blackboard imagery is equally evident in another painting of this group (plate 63), but here the rotating, oval rhythms are replaced by an equally windswept memory of some archetypal, pre-Euclidean geometry lesson, a mental tornado of as yet undisciplined rectangular planes that are occasionally defined further by numbers and letters which, in a more rational world, would fix and measure them precisely. And in the last of this quartet, *Untitled Grey Painting (Bolsena)* of 1969 (plate 67), we are almost back to the tabula rasa except for the tremulous marks of lines that seek out the parallelism of two horizontal axes, and of phantom streaks of paint that recall the marks of chalk erased on the blackboards of our childhood memories. It is fascinating as well to see how these austere, yet spontaneous exercises in reconstructing the origins of calligraphy and geometry bear fruit in both earlier and later works of a more fanciful, free-wheeling character. Thus, the untitled painting of 1969 (plate 65) recaptures, together with other fugitive images, some of the breeze-blown geometries in the more severe painting of 1968 (plate 63). Indeed, like any master, Twombly has created his own universe of forms, a language of metamorphic wisps that not only plunge us deeply into our own most primitive memories, but into the origins of history, myth, civilisation. Abstractly stated, of course, such goals are those shared by some of the greatest artists and thinkers of the first half of our century, such as Miró or Freud; yet when resurrected by Twombly, they seem the most primitive of birthrights, the unique dream of an artist whose precious sensibilities keep eluding mainstream categories.

Peter Schjeldahl   **Andy Warhol**

The full story of Andy Warhol belongs to social rather than to art history, as the tale of a candid soul who had his way with the machinery of fashion that dominates cultural life in America. But art criticism can contribute a reason why the story is worth telling. For a short while, roughly 1962–4, Andy Warhol was a great painter, one of the best in this half of the twentieth century. That his greatness was brief is no mystery: He temporarily gave up painting for film, then, far more than he probably meant to, for the celebrity grind. (Since his transformation from cottage industrialist to socialite small businessman in the late 1960s, his art has sputtered.) What is mysterious is his greatness itself, little discerned and discussed because rarely isolated from the befogging Warhol aura. After two decades of talking around Warhol's real achievement, are we ready, at last, to look at it?

My own conviction about Warhol's work of 1962–4, especially the 'Marilyns' and the 'Disasters', has grown steadily, upped a notch, it seems, every time I see a collection of 1960s art. These paintings occupy the narrow pinnacle of Pop art, certainly; only some Roy Lichtensteins retain a comparably undimmed brilliance. But 'Pop' is a withered category for Warhol's best work. Always more the slogan than the characterisation of a sensibility (unlike 'Minimalist', which makes a point about the art it labels), 'Pop' has come to denote no more than art with sources in popular culture – a definition that needs to be both deepened and transcended in Warhol's case. He is an artist, and a man, with roots in popular culture of exceptional relevance; he was also, for a time, a legitimate heir of modernist tradition. He seamlessly united the low and the high – leading many to embrace the fiction that such seamlessness is an attainable goal, rather than the perishable miracle it proved to be.

The most significant features of Warhol's biography are two: his anomalous (for an American artist) emergence from the lower working class, as the son of an immigrant Czech labourer in Pittsburgh, and his precociously splendid career as a fashion illustrator in the late 1950s. His background gave Warhol an angle on the national culture at once quite ordinary and, from the dominant middle-class viewpoint (shared by all other Pop artists), bizarre. His success in the fashion world added a windfall of historic timing, because it accorded with a moment of rapprochement between art and fashion, when one could step between them without leaping. It was a moment of strong dynamism for American culture as a whole, marked by, among other things, explosive upward social mobility and widespread impatience with middle-class values. Never bourgeois, Warhol ascended from the bottom to the top of the heap without traversing the middle – thus his seemingly angelic or Martian strangeness. He was plunged into refinement with his absolutely sincere vulgarity intact.

Sincerity was the last thing middle-class minds could believe about Warhol, and a lot of us, seeking the key to his cynicism or naïveté, tied ourselves in knots of our own cynical or naïve projections. Like Poe's purloined letter, Warhol hid in plain sight. When he said he liked Coca-Cola, adored movie stars, and was excited by grisly accident reports, he was only giving voice to standard demotic sensibilities. Though sometimes facetious, he has never been truly ironic, because free of the value-conflicts (bane of the bourgeois) that necessitate irony. He was driven by uncomplicated desires for fame and money and, in no way inconsistently, by a yen for artistic glory – 'I want to be Matisse', he said early on, as usual to general incredulity – and the result was something very like Matissean elegance combined with the granting of Warhol's other famous wish, which was to be a machine.

He hit upon his mature style after two years of attempts to iconise the mood of aesthetic fascination with popular culture that was then in the air. Given the quantity and intensity of his experiments, as well as the murderous velocity of the surrounding world, two years was a long time. The brazenly presentational *Campbell's Soup Can* (plate 69), one of dozens made for his first show, in 1962, marks the end of Warhol's experimental phase, which had progressively immersed him in the visual codes of mass-produced images of mass-produced goods. (It is crucial to note that Warhol did not 'paint soup cans' but rather the commercially stylised *images* of soup cans; for him, as for no other artist before him, images were nature.) By being handpainted, however, the pictures had a residual artiness. This was soon effaced by his innovative adoption of photo-transfer silkscreening, in pictures of which the Elvises (plates 71 and 72) and the smashing *Marilyn ×100* (plate 70) were among the first. The device gave full naturalism to the image – as a pre-existing, indefinitely replicatable sign – and opened a tremendous range of pictorial possibilities.

With his subject matter and technique in place, Warhol suddenly let loose a pent-up, profound understanding of New York School painting aesthetics. For effortless command of the grand-scale interaction of shape, size, and colour, Warhol was bettered in his generation only by Frank Stella. Visually and physically, *Marilyn ×100* has majesty reminiscent of Pollock and Newman – comparisons it insouciantly jeers with the nonchalance of its off-registered (in relation to the framing edge) overall image and the widely varying pains taken with each of the hundred faces (piquant inflections of the unbreakable unity of the whole). The effect is like *Moby Dick* retold, to resounding success, in street slang, with a sexy actress standing in for the fearsome white whale. In this version, the movie star is equally a subject of awe – and equally elusive, swimming somewhere beneath fathoms of images of images of images.

That Warhol (again, briefly) had much to say in his new language is proved by his series of Electric Chair and Disaster pictures. They are dark counterpoints to the star-worshipping vicariousness of the Marilyn – its quality of eroticised remoteness, such as a dominant culture displays at its social peripheries. They, too, have class connotations. Capital punishment, violence, and the Saturday-night auto wreck are typically lower-class ways to die – the last-mentioned being relatively more democratic, therefore the more disturbing. (The car-crash pictures sold slowly at the time, while the electric chairs were snapped up.) Again, the sacrosanct field of the New York-type 'big painting' is simultaneously violated and aggrandised, as ghastly content hones beauty to a lacerating edge.

Double Disaster: Silver Car Crash, 1963 (plate 73), is a masterpiece. It comprises two panels sprayed silver, one of them blank and the other bearing an uneven grid of fifteen silkscreened, black, identical images of a grotesque aftermath: A car has demolished itself against a telephone pole; the dead driver slumps in the front seat. The silkscreening is purposefully negligent, with too little or too much medium variously debasing an image already much decayed. Compounded by multiplication and by an asserted equivalence with blank, silver nothingness, the degradation of the image intensifies its deeply obscene character, its terror as a *momento mori* of 'disaster' as a voyeuristic curiosity, of death without dignity. (In our age, is there another kind?)

In what sense is the blank panel another, *double* disaster? The mirror-suggesting silveriness leaves this up to the viewer, as if to say, 'Put yourself in the picture. What is the worst thing you can imagine?' Distanced by a mediating language of calamity on the one hand, we are drawn into inchoate fantasy on the other. The pitiless chill of silver is the weather of the transaction. Its trickiness with light makes the painting at once hard and cloudy, strident and insubstantial – like consciousness, perhaps, under stress. If only consciousness will remember to be strictly aesthetic, the painting insinuates, any horror can be taken in stride, even savoured. Now, *poètes maudits* have always told us as much, but never with this complicitous directness that makes everyday, middling-sensual *poètes maudits* of us all. Morally, Warhol's art of this period is about going to the ends of aestheticism as a matter of routine.

After the supreme tension of the Disasters, Warhol's inspiration slackened, though he maintained a high level through 1964 and continued to produce good pictures with existing screens rather longer. His ravishing 'Flowers' (plate 80) were a kind of concentrated essence of the new beauty Warhol had discovered through his silkscreen process, and they marked the sunset of his painting activity. Later he resumed painting and print-making, and he has done many series since, at least one of them marvellous: His giant 'Maos' of the early 1970s (plate 83), candy-coloured evocations of the totalitarian sublime, wittily emblematised that time's political susceptibilities and its revised interest in 'expressive' painterliness. But Warhol's sense of live social and artistic matters was increasingly muffled. Wealth and fame, possessed, took possession of their possessor. Barring yet another comeback, Warhol's last work of much interest was a workmanlike series of standard-format portraits of the rich and famous.

Like most major modern artists, the halcyon Warhol was both radical and conservative, looking both forward and backward in cultural time. He (1) inserted painting in a humiliating semiotic continuum as one medium among many of the mass culture, and (2) made great paintings. Initially appearing to ridicule the preciousness of art with a technique of mass production, Warhol and his silkscreening – actually a clumsy and messy artisan device – finally mocked mass production and exalted painting. This was possible because, for a while, he was onto something serious: chaos – systems entropy, human madness and death – as a crack in the world through which could be glimpsed a violent bliss. It was only a glimpse, but its after-image will linger for as long as Warhol's best paintings are shown and seen.

Plates

Dimensions are given first in inches, then in
centimetres.
Height precedes width precedes depth, unless
otherwise indicated.

RICHARD ARTSCHWAGER

1
Mirror Painting
1962
Acrylic on celotex, formica and wood
60 × 31 × 10 (153 × 79 × 25)

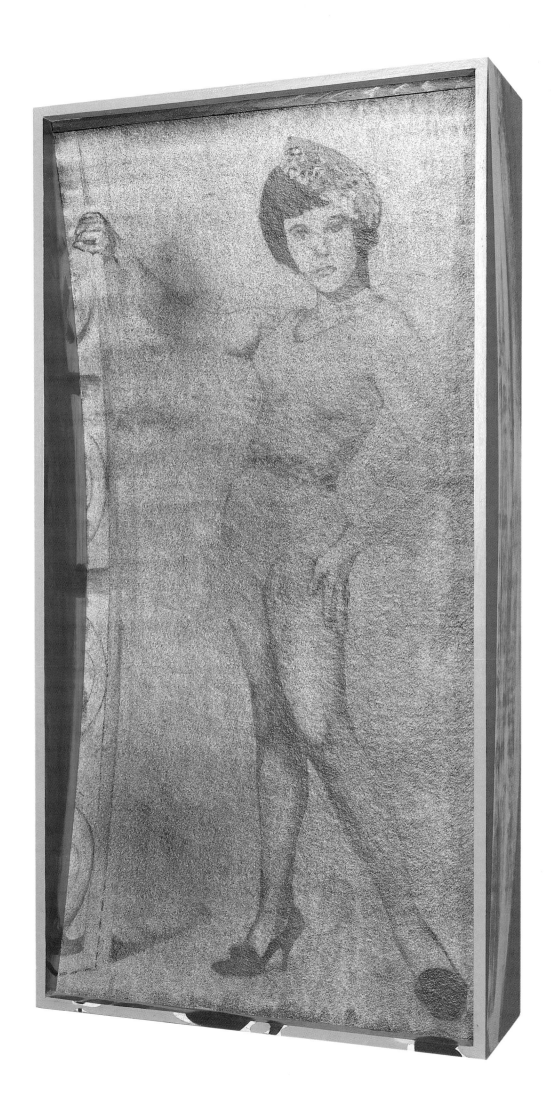

RICHARD ARTSCHWAGER

2
Rocker I
1964
Formica on plywood, steel counterweight
62 ×26 ×28 (157 ×65 ×72)

RICHARD ARTSCHWAGER

3
Table with Pink Tablecloth
1964
Formica on wood
25¼ ×44 ×44 (64 ×112 ×112)

Rocker I
1964
Formica on plywood, steel counterweight
62 ×26 ×28 (157 ×65 ×72)

Table with Pink Tablecloth
1964
Formica on wood
25¼ ×44 ×44 (64 ×112 ×112)

RICHARD ARTSCHWAGER

4
Mirror
1964
Formica
61 × 43 × 4 (155 × 110 × 10)

RICHARD ARTSCHWAGER

5
Long Table with Two Pictures
1964
Table: Formica on wood
33¾ ×96 ×22¼ (86 ×244 ×56)
Pictures: Acrylic on celotex with formica
Each: 42 ×32¼ (107 ×82)

RICHARD ARTSCHWAGER

6
Handle
1965
Formica
42½×13×12 (108×33×31)

RICHARD ARTSCHWAGER

7
Chair
1966
Formica
59×18×30 (151×46×77)

RICHARD ARTSCHWAGER

8
Expression Impression
1966
Acrylic on celotex
23 ½ × 30 (60 × 76)

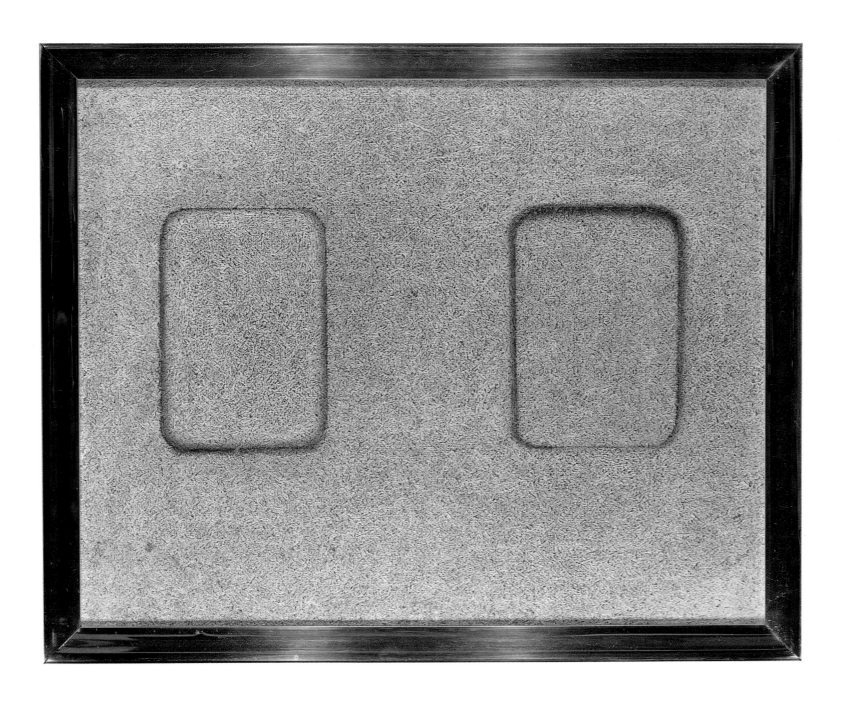

RICHARD ARTSCHWAGER

9
Office Scene
1966
Acrylic on celotex
42 × 43 (106·7 × 109)

RICHARD ARTSCHWAGER

10
Upper Right Corner Hit
1969
Acrylic on celotex
23½ × 30 (60 × 76)

RICHARD ARTSCHWAGER

11
Bushes II
1970
Acrylic on celotex
23 1/2 × 28 1/4 (60 × 72)

RICHARD ARTSCHWAGER

12
Library
1965
Acrylic on celotex
30×41 (76×104)

RICHARD ARTSCHWAGER

13
Untitled Interior
1973
Acrylic on celotex
60×46⅝ (152·4×118·4)

RICHARD ARTSCHWAGER

14 **Interior (North)** 1973 Acrylic on celotex
2 panels: Top 52¾×88½ (134×225) Bottom 52⅛×88½ (133×225)

RICHARD ARTSCHWAGER

15 **Interior (West)** 1973 Acrylic on celotex
2 panels: Top 48⅞×75⅞ (124×193) Bottom 50⅞×75⅞ (129·5×193)

RICHARD ARTSCHWAGER

16
Eight Rat Holes
1968/75
Acrylic on celotex
8 panels: (1) 23½×19 (59·5×48·5)
          (2) 18×23 (45·5×58)
          (3) 18×24 (46×61)
          (4) 23×18 (58·5×46)
          (5) 23×22 (58·5×56)
          (6) 23×19 (58·5×48·5)
          (7) 22×24 (56×61)
          (8) 28½×23 (72·5×58)

RICHARD ARTSCHWAGER

17
Tower III (Confessional)
1980
Formica and oak
60×47×32 (153×120×81)

RICHARD ARTSCHWAGER

18
Book II (Nike)
1981
Formica
74 ×45¾ ×46 (188 ×116 ×117)

RICHARD ARTSCHWAGER

19
Rug and Window
1983
Acrylic on celotex
51½ ×51¾ (131 ×132)

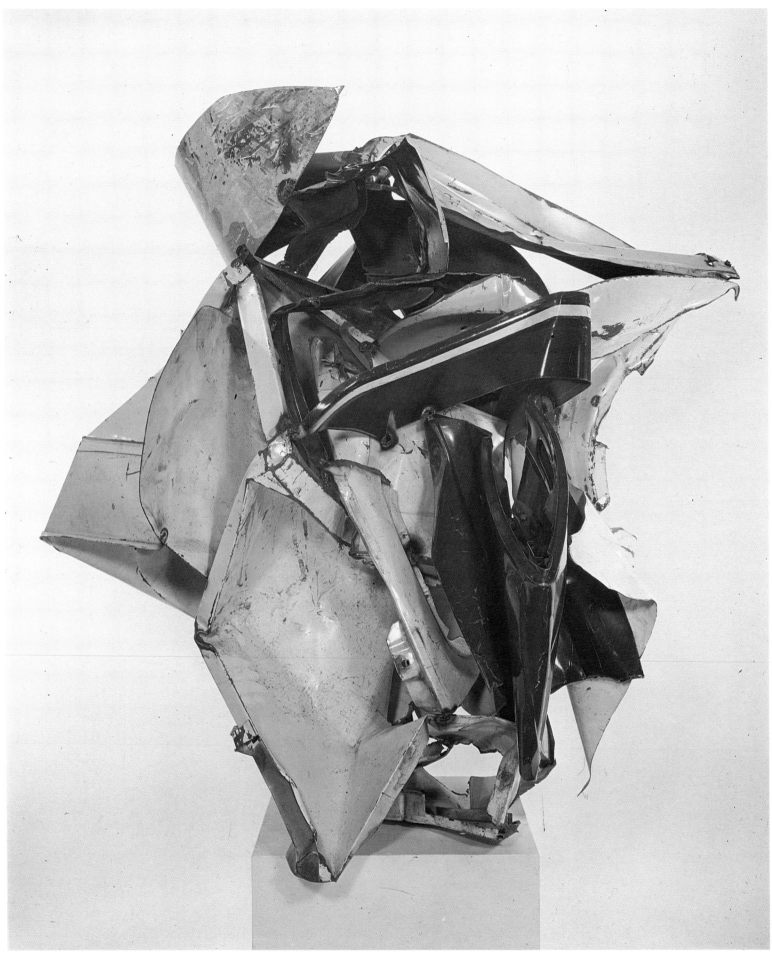

JOHN CHAMBERLAIN

20 **Captain O'Hay** 1961
Welded auto metal 45 (114) high

JOHN CHAMBERLAIN

21 **Pure Drop** 1982
Painted and chromium plated steel
135 ×72 ×36 (343 ×183 ×91·5)

JOHN CHAMBERLAIN

22
The Arch of Lumps (two views)
1983
Painted and chromium plated steel
142 ×64 ×57 ½ (360·7 ×162·6 ×146)

JOHN CHAMBERLAIN

23
Fenollosa's Column (two views)
1983
Painted and chromium plated steel
125½×53×47½ (318·8×134·6×120·7)

LUCAS SAMARAS

24
Untitled – October 23, 1960
1960
Pastel on paper
Sheet: 12 ×9 (30·5 ×23)

LUCAS SAMARAS

25
Untitled – February 16, 1961
1961
Pastel on paper
Sheet: 12×9 (30·5×23)

LUCAS SAMARAS

26
Untitled – August 14, 1961
1961
Pastel on paper
Sheet: 12 ×9 (30·5 ×23)

LUCAS SAMARAS

27
Untitled – August 14, 1961
1961
Pastel on paper
Sheet: 12 ×9 (30·5 ×23)

LUCAS SAMARAS

26
Untitled – August 14, 1961
1961
Pastel on paper
Sheet: 12 ×9 (30·5 ×23)

LUCAS SAMARAS

27
Untitled – August 14, 1961
1961
Pastel on paper
Sheet: 12 ×9 (30·5 ×23)

LUCAS SAMARAS

28
Untitled – Early November 1961
1961
Pastel on paper
Sheet: 12 × 9 (30·5 × 23)

LUCAS SAMARAS

29
Untitled – July 13, 1962
1962
Pastel on paper
Sheet: 12 × 9 (30·5 × 23)

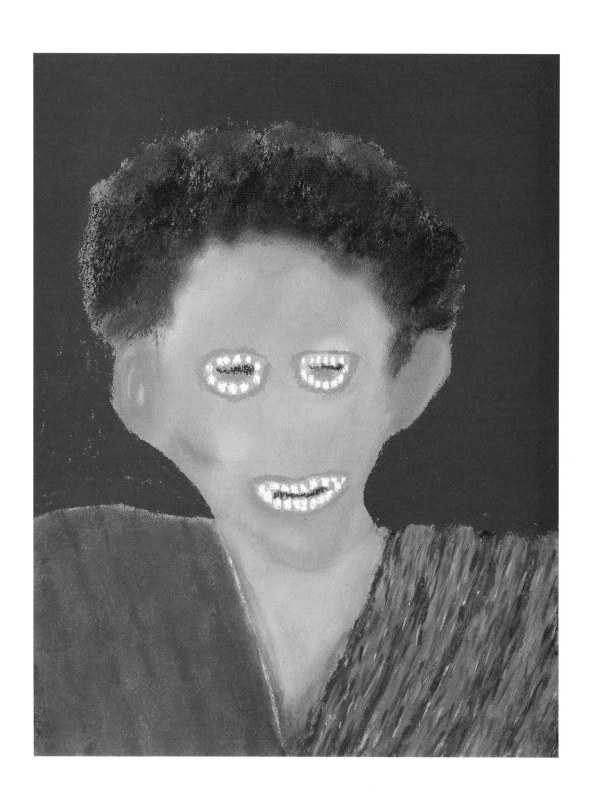

LUCAS SAMARAS

30
Untitled – July 17, 1962
1962
Pastel on paper
Sheet: 12 ×9 (30·5 ×23)

LUCAS SAMARAS

31
Box No.4
1963
Wood construction, steel straight pins, nails,
hinges, razor blades, fork, plastic, sand, glass plate
and goblet, mosaic tiles, coloured wool yarn
Open: 18¼ ×24½ ×11½ (46·5 ×62·5 ×29·7)

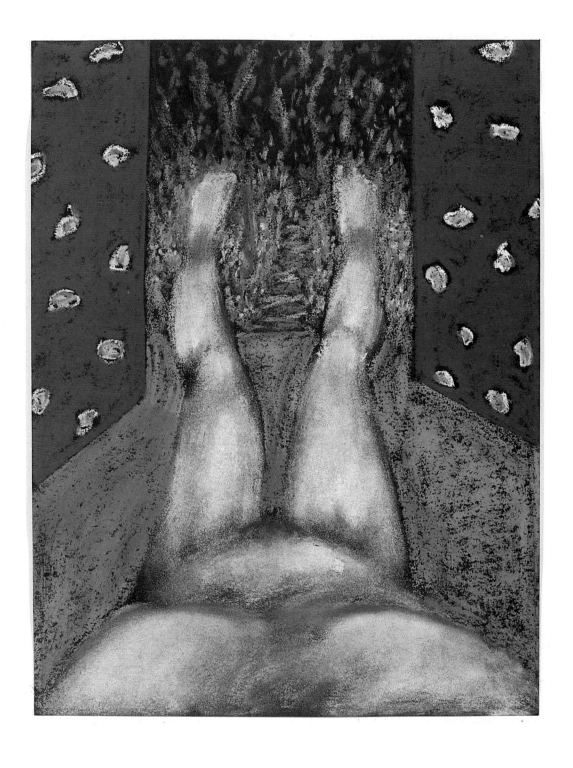

LUCAS SAMARAS

32
Box No.8 (two views)
1963
Wood construction, wool yarn, photographs, wire,
glass lenses, plastic, stuffed bird
Closed: 11 ×15 ×8 (28 ×38 ×20)

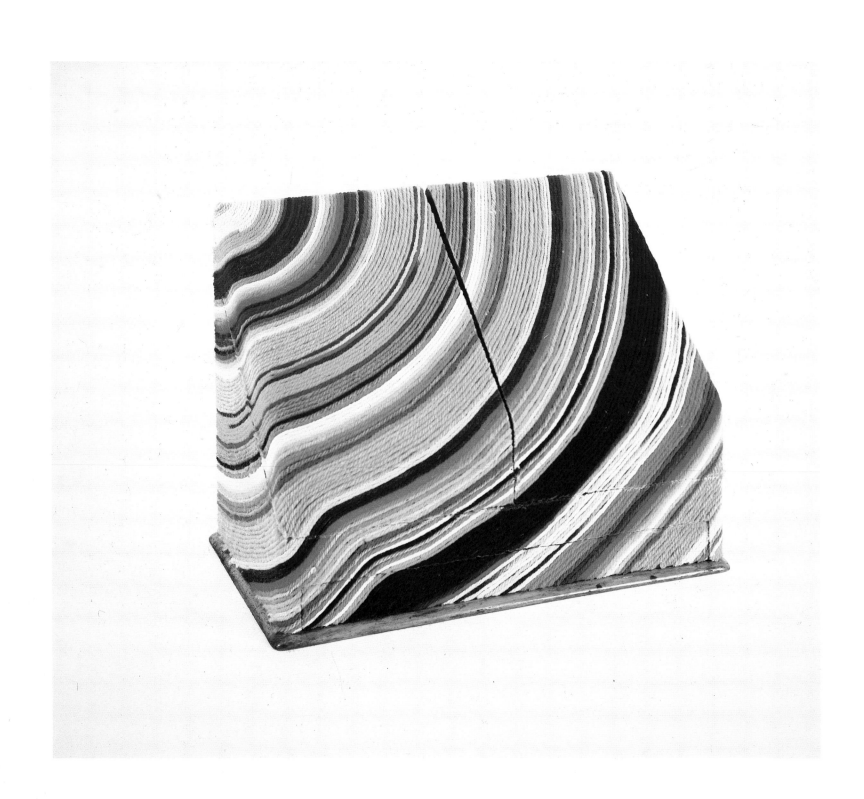

LUCAS SAMARAS

33
Self Portrait Box
1963
Wood construction, red-white-blue wool yarn, steel
straight pins, 50 photographs of the artist, lead piece
Closed: 3¾×5⅞×4⅜ (9·5×15×11·2)

LUCAS SAMARAS

34
Shoe Box
1965
Wood construction, wool yarn, shoe, steel straight
pins, cotton, paint
10½ × 15½ × 11 (26·7 × 39·4 × 28)

LUCAS SAMARAS

35
Box No.49 (two views)
1966
Wood construction, wool yarn, beads, plexiglass, plastic
Closed: 5 × 12 × 9 (13 × 30·5 × 23)

LUCAS SAMARAS

35a
Chair Transformation No.20
1969/70
Corten steel
95 × 18 × 19 (241·3 × 45·7 × 48·3)

LUCAS SAMARAS

36
Room No.3
1968
Mirror on wood frame
108×108×108 (274×274×274)

Detail of interior

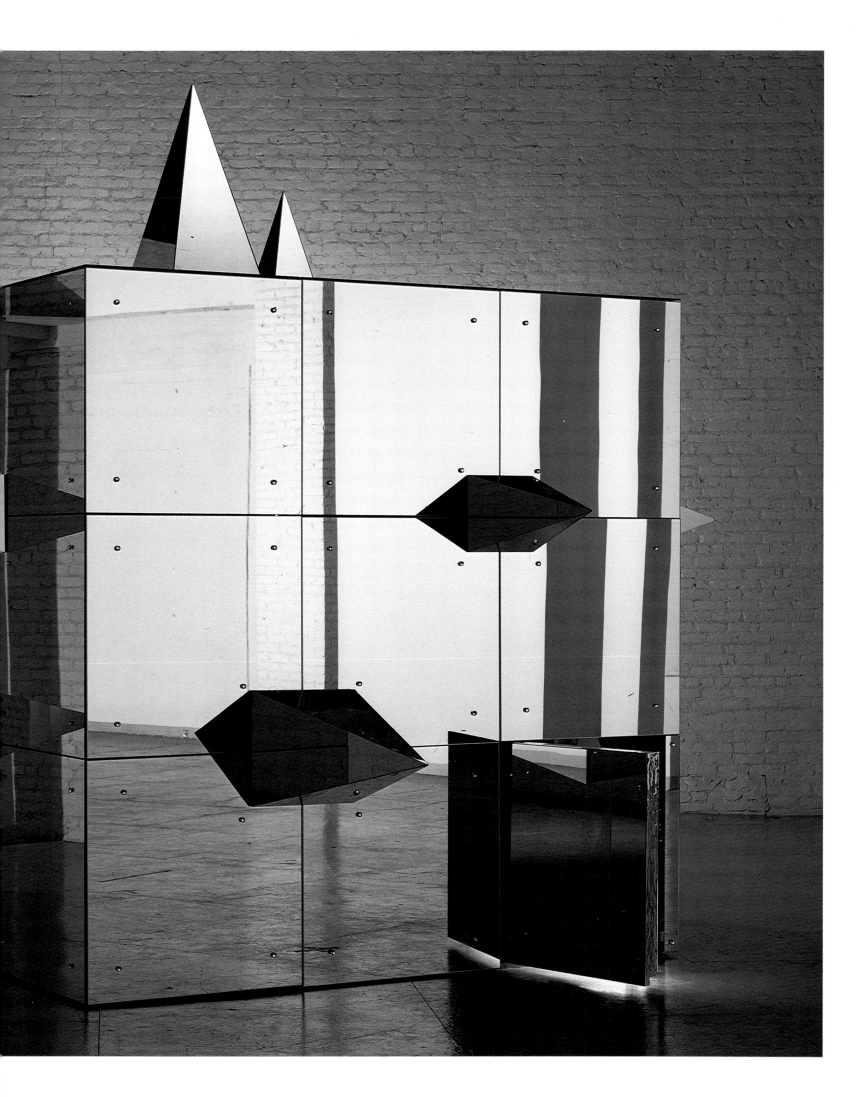

LUCAS SAMARAS

37
Chicken Wire Box No.21
1972
Acrylic on chicken wire mesh
13⁷/₈×11³/₄×15 (35×30×38)

LUCAS SAMARAS

38
10/25/73
1973
SX 70 Polaroid
3 × 3 (7·6 × 7·6)

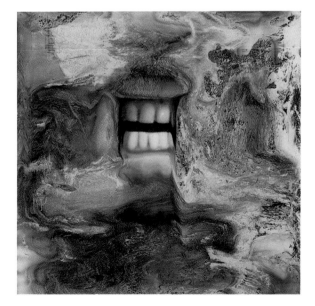

LUCAS SAMARAS

39
11/1/73
1973
SX 70 Polaroid
3 × 3 (7·6 × 7·6)

LUCAS SAMARAS

40
4/4/76
1976
SX 70 Polaroid
3 ×3 (7·6 ×7·6)

LUCAS SAMARAS

41
4/4/76
1976
SX 70 Polaroid
3 ×3 (7·6 ×7·6)

LUCAS SAMARAS

42
7/31/76
1976
SX 70 Polaroid
3 × 3 (7·6 × 7·6)

LUCAS SAMARAS

43
9/8/76
1976
SX 70 Polaroid
3 × 3 (7·6 × 7·6)

LUCAS SAMARAS

44
Box No.82
1976
Wood construction, steel straight pins, sculpmetal,
paint
17×12×10½ (43×30·5×27)

LUCAS SAMARAS

45
Box No.94
1976
Wood construction, wool yarn, steel straight pins,
acrylic, knives
13×13×26 (33×33×66)

LUCAS SAMARAS

46
Sculpture Table
1981
Gold plated bronze
41¾×51½×35 (106×131×89)

LUCAS SAMARAS

47
Sculpture Table
1981
Silver plated bronze
41¾×51½×35 (106×131×89)

LUCAS SAMARAS

48
Chair with Male – Female Entanglement II
1983
Gold plated bronze
33 × 17½ × 19 (83·8 × 44·5 × 48·3)

LUCAS SAMARAS

49
Head Group No.3
1983
Ink wash on paper
22 sheets, Overall: 96 × 132 (243·8 × 335·3)

FRANK STELLA

50
Joatinga I
1975
Lacquer and oil on aluminium
96 × 132 (240 × 330)

FRANK STELLA

51
Steller's Albatross
1976
Mixed media on aluminium
120×165 (304·8×419)

FRANK STELLA

52
Laysan Millerbird
1977
Mixed media on aluminium
83 × 123 × 15 (207·5 × 307·5 × 37·5)

FRANK STELLA

53
Thruxton
1982
Mixed media on etched magnesium
109½×110¾×23 (273·8×277×57·5)

FRANK STELLA

54 (following page)
President Brand
1982
Honeycomb aluminium
121×101×78 (302·5×252·5×195)

55 (following page)
Western Driefontein
1982
Aluminium and etched magnesium with mixed media
120×100×80 (304·8×254×203)

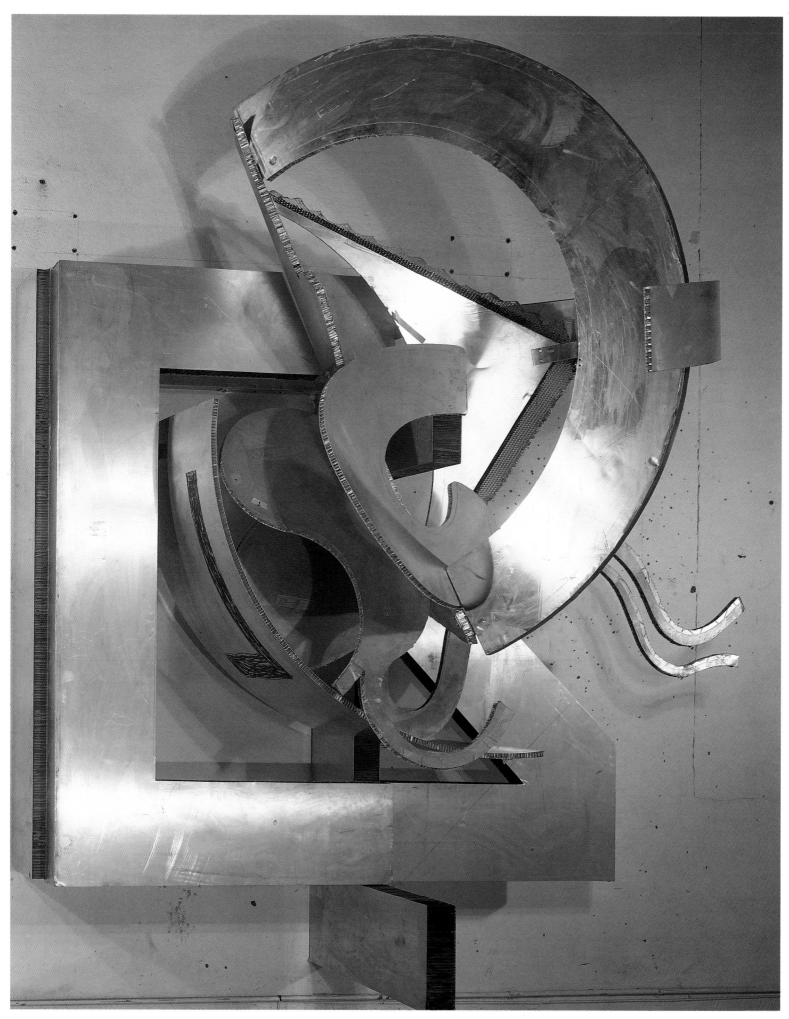

FRANK STELLA

56
Western Holdings (three views)
1983
Mixed media on aluminium
120 × 112 × 98 (304·8 × 280 × 245)

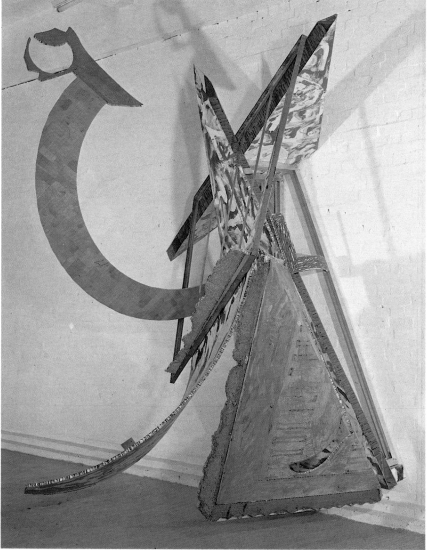

CY TWOMBLY

57
Untitled
1956
Oil, crayon, pencil on canvas
48¹⁄₈×69 (122·2×175·3)

CY TWOMBLY

57a
Untitled
1959
Oil, crayon, pencil on canvas
58 ×79 (147 ×200)

58
Leda and the Swan
1960
Oil, crayon, pencil on canvas
76¼×80 (190·5×203)

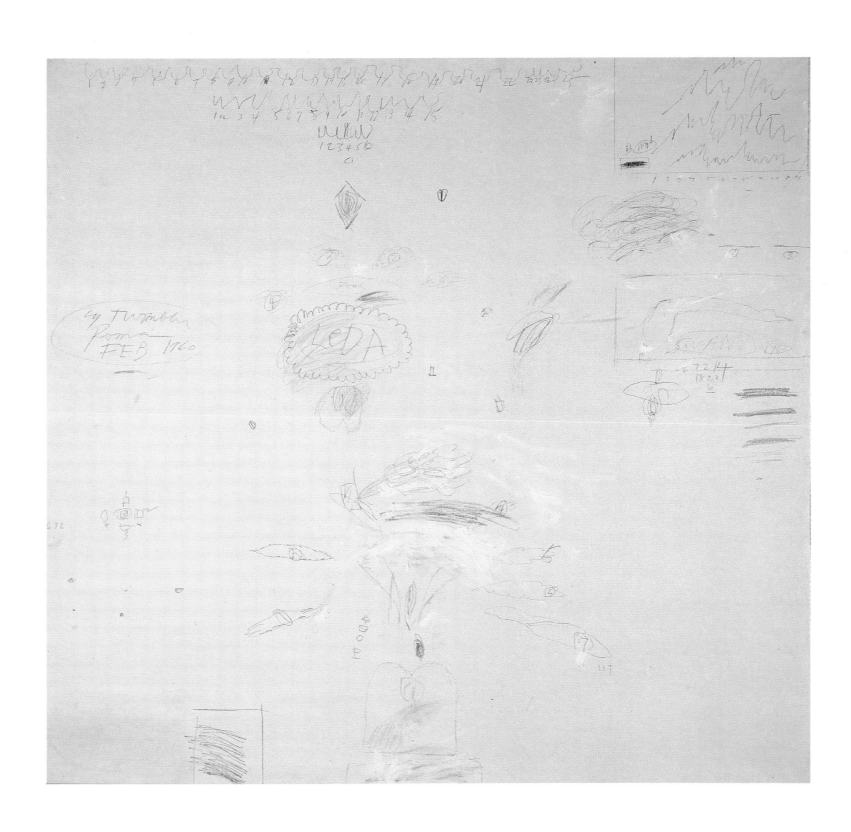

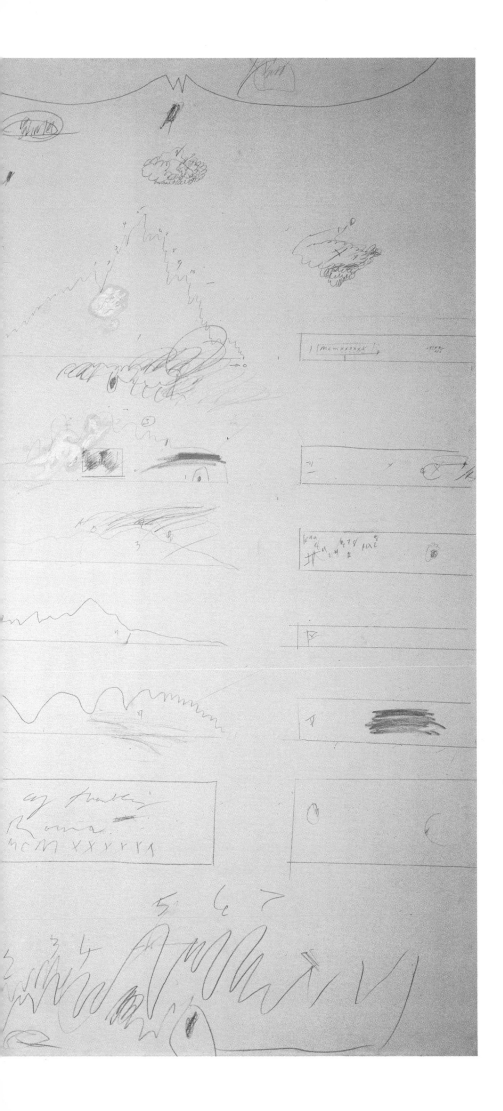

CY TWOMBLY

59
Sahara
1960
Oil, crayon, pencil on canvas
80×110 (203×275)

CY TWOMBLY

60
Red Painting
1961
Oil, crayon, pencil on canvas
66×80 (165×203)

CY TWOMBLY

61
A Roma
1964
House paint, crayon, pencil on canvas
78¾×82½ (200×206·3)

CY TWOMBLY

62
Untitled
1968
House paint, crayon on canvas
68×90 (170×225)

CY TWOMBLY

63
Untitled
1968
Oil, crayon on canvas
60×68 (150×170)

CY TWOMBLY

64
Untitled
1968
Oil, pencil on canvas
68⅛ ×87⅞ (173 ×216)

CY TWOMBLY

65
Untitled (Bolsena)
1969
House paint, oil, crayon, pencil on canvas
78¾×98½ (200×250)

CY TWOMBLY

66
Untitled (Bolsena)
1969
House paint, oil, crayon, pencil on canvas
78³⁄₄×98¹⁄₂ (200×250)

CY TWOMBLY

67
Untitled Grey Painting (Bolsena)
1969
Oil, crayon on canvas
78¾×98½ (200×250)

ANDY WARHOL

69
Campbell's Soup Can
1962
Oil on canvas
20 × 16 (50·8 × 40·6)

ANDY WARHOL

70
Marilyn ×100
1962
Acrylic and silkscreen on canvas
81 ×223½ (205·7 ×567·7)

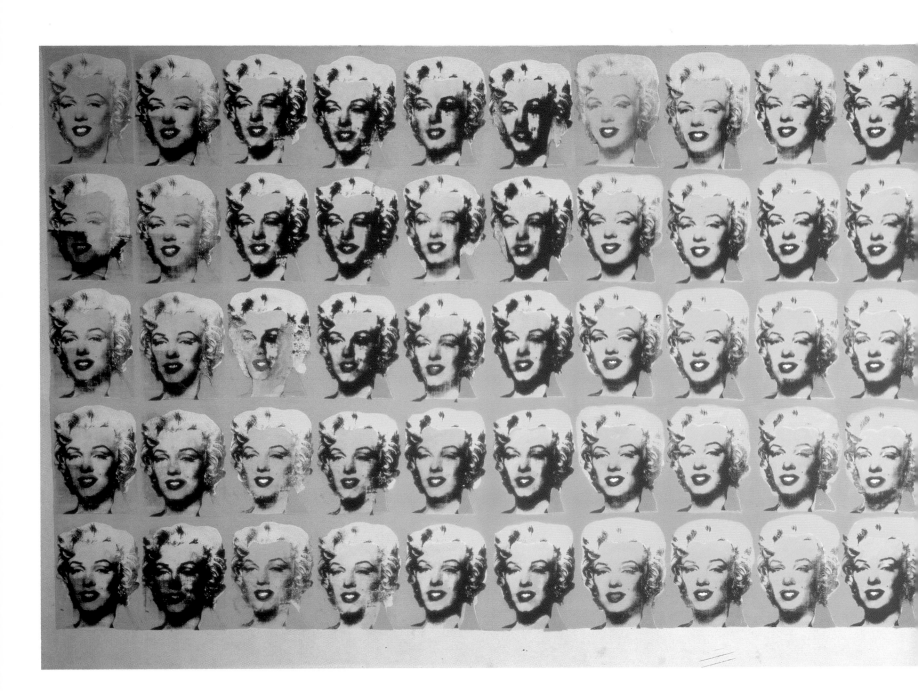

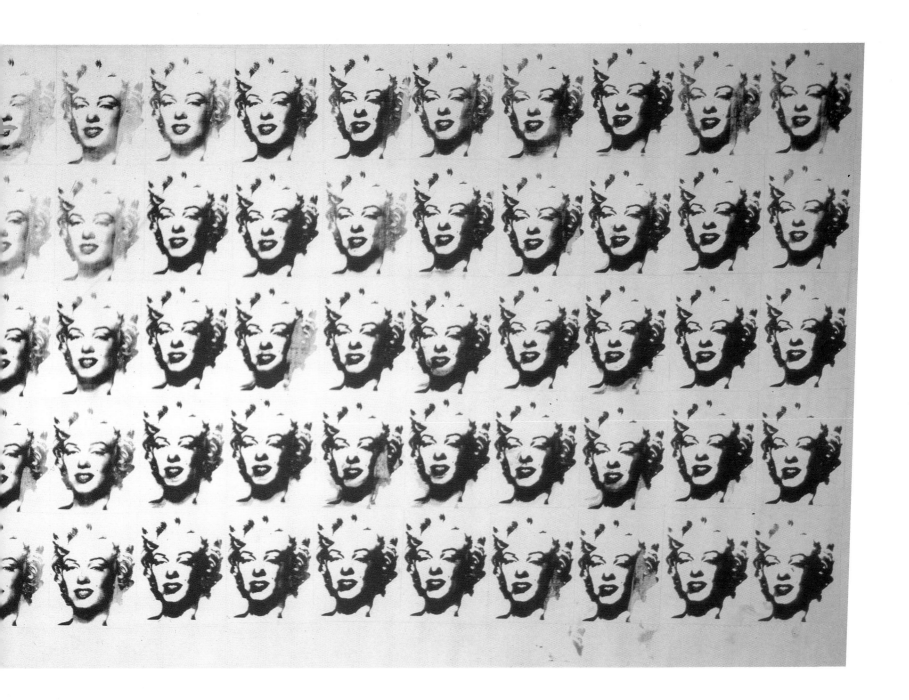

ANDY WARHOL

71
Triple Elvis
1962
Acrylic silkscreened on canvas
82×118 (208·3×299·7)

ANDY WARHOL

72
Elvis 49 Times
1962
Acrylic and silkscreen on canvas
80½×60 (204·5×152·4)

ANDY WARHOL

73 (following pages)
Double Disaster: Silver Car Crash
1963
Silkscreen on canvas
2 panels: 105×166 (266·7×421·6)

ANDY WARHOL

74 (following pages)
Blue Electric Chair
1963
Acrylic and silkscreen on canvas
2 panels: 105×160½ (266·7×407·6)

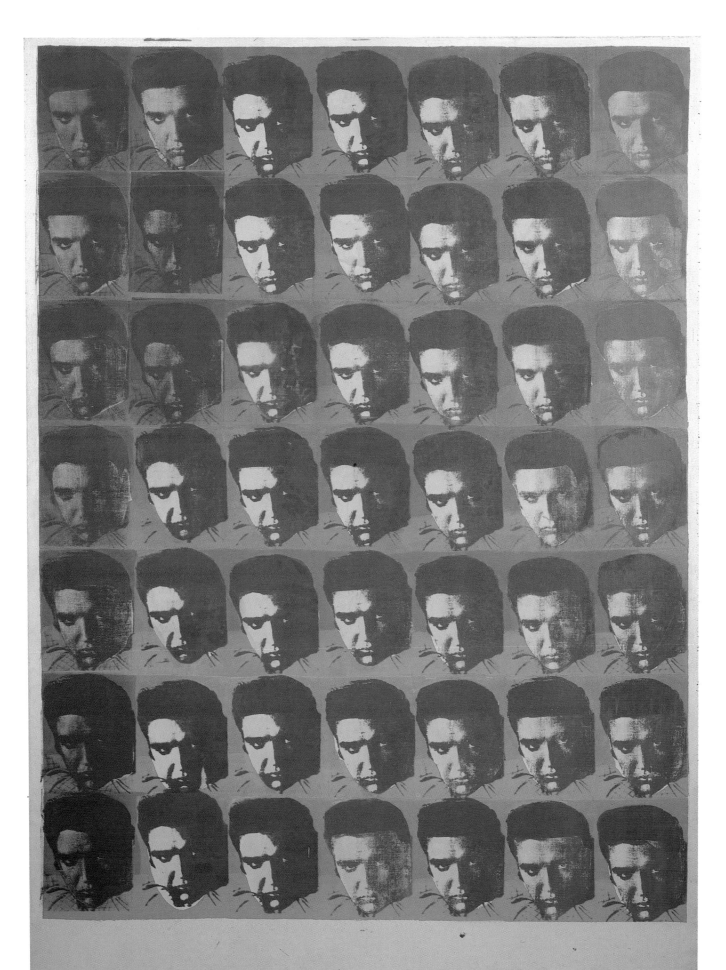

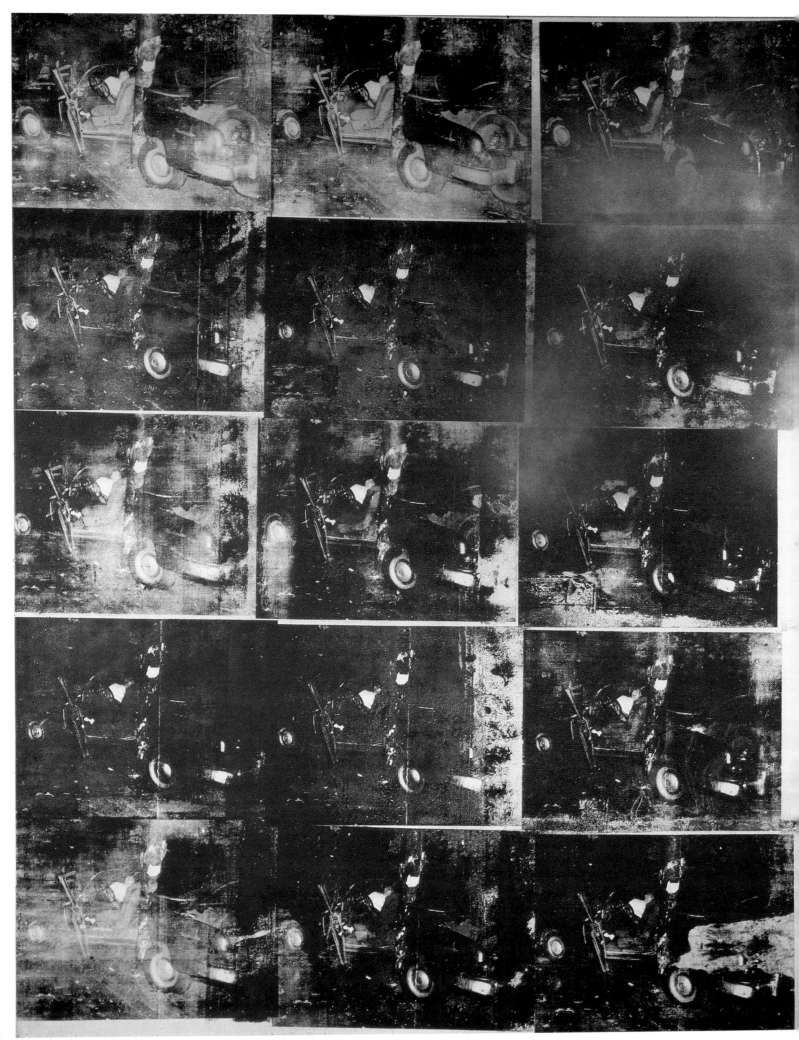

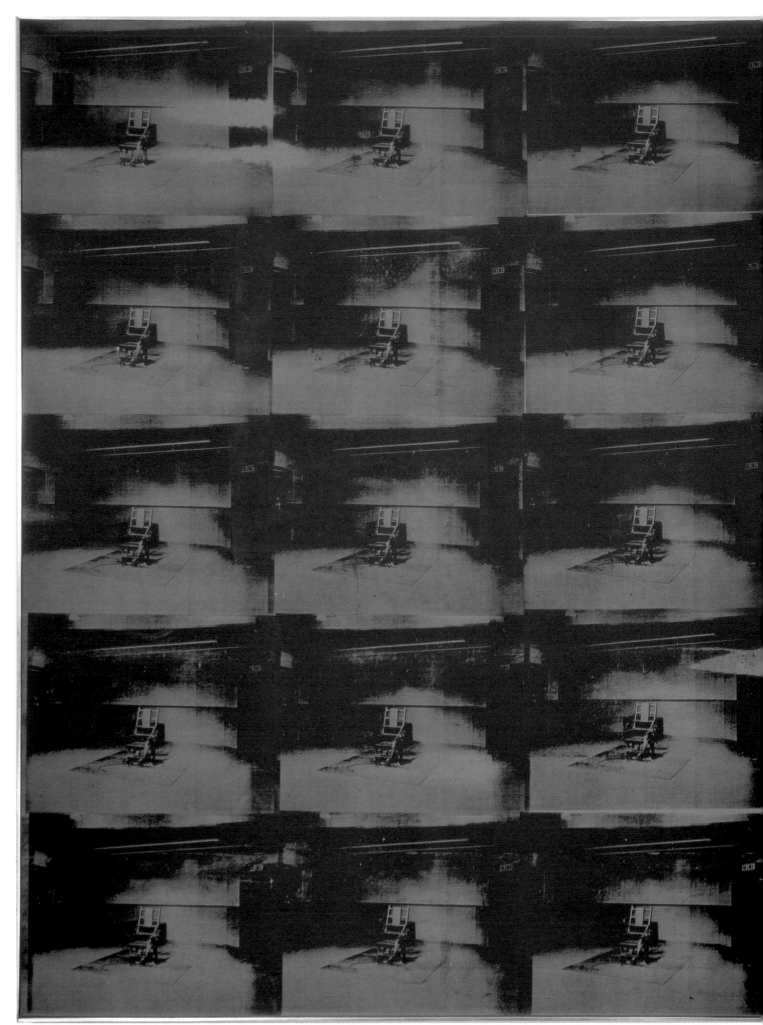

Seized shipment: Did a leak kill . . . Seized shipment: Did a leak kill . . . Seized shipment: Did a leak kill . . .

Seized shipment: Did a leak kill . . Seized shipment: Did a leak kill . . Seized shipment: Did a leak kill . .

Seized shipment: Did a leak kill . . Seized shipment: Did a leak kill . . Seized shipment: Did a leak kill . . .

ANDY WARHOL

75
Tunafish Disaster
1963
Synthetic polymer paint and silkscreen on canvas
124³/₈ ×83 (316 ×211)

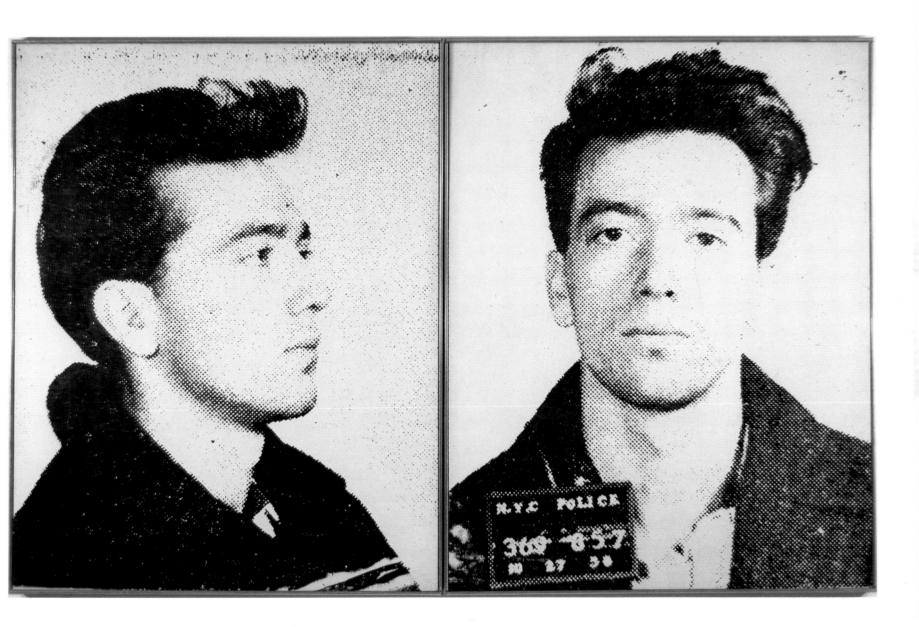

ANDY WARHOL

76
Most Wanted Man No.11, John Joseph H.
1963
Silkscreen on canvas
2 panels: 48 ×80 (122 ×203·2)

ANDY WARHOL

77
Liz
1964
Synthetic polymer paint and silkscreen on canvas
40×40 (101·6×101·6)

ANDY WARHOL

78
Jackie
1965
Synthetic polymer paint and silkscreen on canvas
16 panels: 80×64 (203·2×162·6)

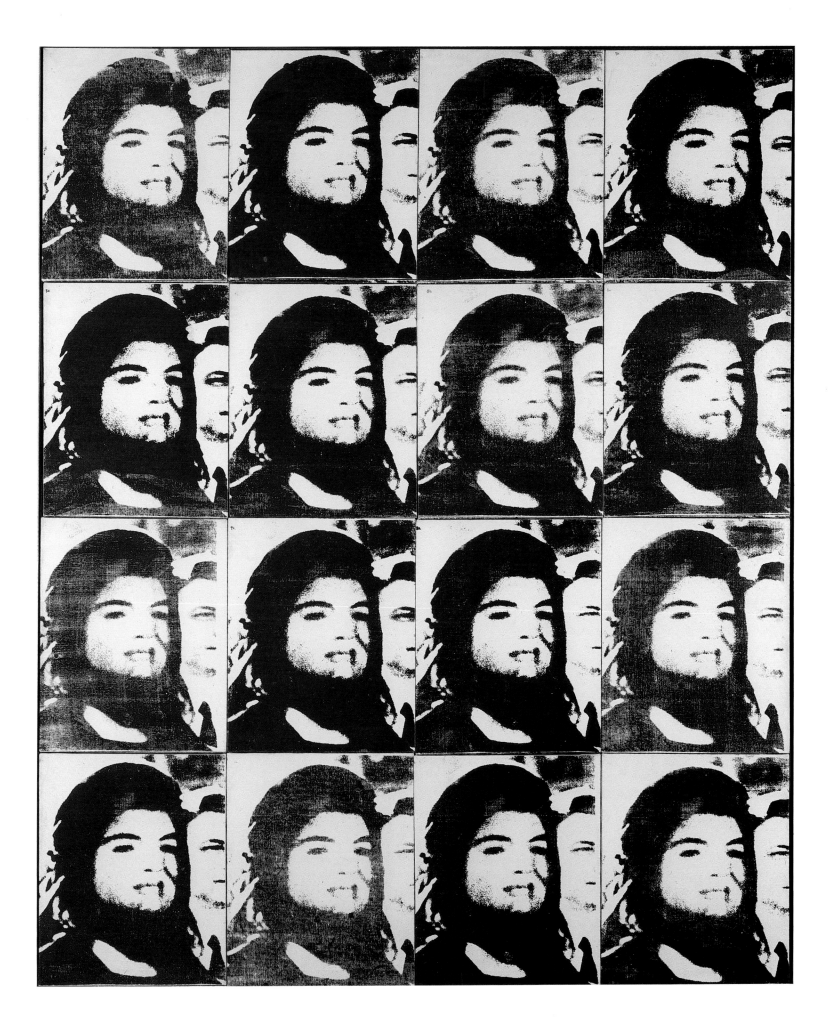

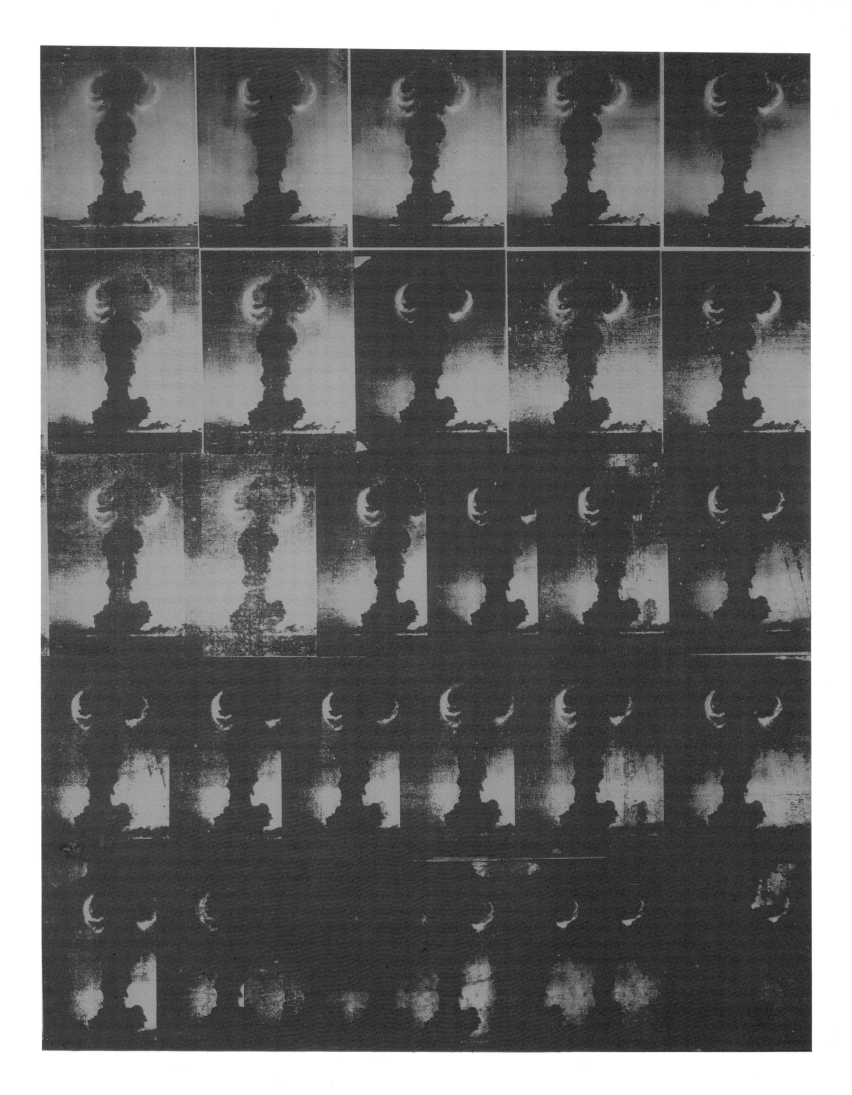

ANDY WARHOL

79
Atomic Bomb
1965
Silkscreen on canvas
104 ×80½ (264 ×204·5)

ANDY WARHOL

80
Flowers
1966
Acrylic and silkscreen enamel on canvas
81¾ ×140½ (207·6 ×356·9)

ANDY WARHOL

81
Double Marlon
1966
Printers ink silkscreened on canvas
84 ×95¾ (213·4 ×243·2)

ANDY **WARHOL**

82
Self Portrait
1967
Acrylic and silkscreen on canvas
72×72 (183×183)

ANDY WARHOL

83 (following page)
Mao
1973
Acrylic and silkscreen on canvas
176½×136¼ (448·3×346·1)